SPIRIT, MY SECOND HOME

To Paul
Andrea
and family
love Rocco
and lots of spiritual success
Bryc 1994

By the same author
Just A Touch Away
I'm Here Listening

SPIRIT, MY SECOND HOME

by

BRYAN GIBSON

Regency Press (London & New York) Ltd.
125 High Holborn, London WC1V 6QA

ISBN 0 7212 0819 3

Printed and bound in Great Britain by
Buckland Press Ltd., Dover, Kent.

Thanks to:

Running Foot, my spirit family and friends,
for their help and guidance.

The families of those mentioned in the book.

Very special thanks to Monica Harrison
for her help and typing her fingers to the bone,
and translating my often nonsensical script!

BRYAN.

CONTENTS

CONTENTS (continued)

LIST OF ILLUSTRATIONS

Page

FAREWELL, MY FRIEND

Farewell, my friend
I will see you again.
The days were sweet,
My heart was warmed,
Your eyes were bright,
And for a magic moment
Life was good.

The road winds on
And we must go
Our separate ways.
The tears have dried
For what we had
Is not to be denied
For it was love.

Love of a greater sort
Than usually meant,
For I am Love
And you are Love
And love reached out
To Love.

But our roads are separate now
And life goes on.
You must tread your way
And I my own;
They both are joy
For in our hearts
We know the Path
And it is good.

Farewell, my friend,
We will meet again,
For you and I have known
What it is to fuse our finer selves
On a plane other than this one.

Wave me a wave with confidence
And smile me a smile as you go
With your black eyes bright
In the summer light
For all that is now has been
And all that has been, is now.

Worlds within worlds
And lives beyond lives
And echoes of future and past
Shimmer between us along the way
And come full-circle at last.

MONICA HARRISON

Chapter One

SPIRIT, MY SECOND HOME

As a spiritually-aware medium, it is nice to be able to say, "Yes, I have two homes." I am lucky. Here, on a material level, I am able to share my home with my family and friends and also have access to a second home in the world of spirit.

From that world come the many voices sending messages to loved ones, telling of their safe arrival in the spirit world and describing happy reunions with relatives and friends who had arrived ahead of them. They want to let us know they are not lost and alone, and have found their new world full of love, peace and harmony, qualities which, in many cases, were missing from their lives here on the earth plane.

Because I am able to see and hear these people now residing in the world of spirit, hopefully I can tell their loved ones here about them, reassuring family and friends that they continue to exist and have settled happily into their new environment. They not only send their love, but communicate their thoughts, often showing us that they still survive by their awareness of situations and problems that have arisen since their unexpected departure into spirit. They will try to offer guidance and put us on the right pathway, but they will not come and live our lives for us. Our loved ones in spirit can guide us and reassure us as to the wisdom of our plans, but the decision making must be ours. It is not for them, nor the medium to make our decisions for us. That is our job.

Eventually, we shall make that transition into the spirit world like those before us, and arrive at our second home. We shall then be able to pass on what we have seen and learned, knowing that we always have contact with the loved ones we have left behind, until the time when we all meet up again in spirit at a later date.

So, really, we never lose out, do we? Everything is just a distance away, although, sadly, we find this very hard to accept. For those of us on the earth plane, the period of waiting and longing to meet up with these special people in the spirit world seems a life-time away, yet really it is just around the corner.

My life began in July 1938. I was born in a farm cottage in the small village of Claypole, near Newark, to Elsie Doris and Clifford Charles Gibson. Sadly, I seem to have very few vivid memories of my early childhood. As I grew up in Claypole, I always felt aware that I was perhaps not the same as others of my own age group and felt very different from them in some ways. Especially, I remember always being more comfortable in the company of the older generation in the village rather than with those my own age.

For a short time, the family moved to a village a few miles away called Brandon, and I can just recall this, although it only lasted for about three years. By this time, the family had increased and I now had a sister called Sheila and a brother, Neville. As I remember, we moved back to Claypole just as I was about to start school.

The family home was now a semi-detached house in Doddington Lane, not far from where I was born. My father was self-employed, working on the land and he decided to buy the house – a big undertaking at the time – and my sister, Jenny, had joined the family by then too. My parents still live in the house, nearly fifty years later.

Our next-door neighbour, Mrs. Sleaford, is one of the most impressive people I remember from the village in my childhood days. She lived in a large, detached house. This sad, rather unusual, lady was very eccentric. She never bothered much about her appearance and would always wear clothes on top of clothes. Although a very small lady, she always seemed twice the size because of this and, without being unkind, she was not a person you would wish to stand near on a hot day. I think most of the village people regarded her as slightly strange, as she was seen very often talking to herself, and her behaviour was somewhat reclusive.

Mrs. Sleaford's house was hidden by a very large hedge, which I don't think was ever cut. No one was ever allowed into the house. If you went to the door, it would only open a very small way and a head would appear around the door. As she kept cats, the aroma was sometimes quite strong. Quite often, when you called at the door, she wouldn't answer at all although you knew she was there and would be aware of her behind the curtains. My sister, Jenny, was always afraid when it was her turn to call there, and would run all the way to get it over with quickly.

For the times when Mrs. Sleaford called at our house, a special cup was kept which was never used by anyone else but her. To me, this unusual, special lady was fascinating. I always got on well with her and was never afraid of her, often doing errands and shopping for her whenever she asked me.

I suppose Mrs. Sleaford never really treated me as a child and would sometimes surprise me with a bus trip to Grantham followed by a visit to the local theatre – a treat which in those days was definitely something special.

Looking back, I feel perhaps Mrs. Sleaford was a spiritually-aware person who never really understood it, and no doubt faced difficulties and ridicule by not fitting into a normal family life and situation. However, knowing this rather unusual and, to me, special lady, is something I can look back on and appreciate.

I also have some very strong, happy memories of the many days during school holidays when I would wander in the woods by myself, totally at peace, allowing myself to be part of nature, lost in the quiet surroundings with only the birds and wildlife at play in their natural environment. I would daydream, imagining myself one of them for hours at a time, much to the frustration of my mother who did not know where I had disappeared to, faced with my forgotten errands. As all my mother's family lived in our village and I was the first child of my generation in the family, I was lucky, spending a lot of my school years with different aunts and uncles until they began their own families.

By the time I reached double figures, I was living with my grandparents, Maria and George Noon, in a row of houses near the railway station, my grandfather having worked on the railway all his life. Once more, I was living in an environment with a much older generation. I did not find it easy to relate always to my grandma, who could sometimes be very difficult, but I was always spoilt by my grandfather. His one pleasure was to have a bet on the horses and I therefore came to know quite a lot about the racing game. Most Saturdays, he would give me two shillings to place on a horse and most often he said it had won or been well placed, so I got some extra pocket money, but I think he mostly made up the winnings.

My father's father sadly died when I was about eight years old and so I knew very little of him, although I remember he always smoked a pipe. My grandmother was what I would call "a proper granny", small and rounded and I became very close to her as I grew into my teens. I would tell her all my problems and would always try to make an excuse to visit her on a Sunday, especially for her cooking! As we lived only a bike ride away in the next village, we were very lucky to have Granny Gibson live long enough to just see her "nineties".

Looking back, I suppose my childhood was unusual in that I had not been brought up closely with my brother and sisters. Perhaps I missed out on the unity of a family, but my upbringing developed the individuality which is now so much the basis of my character.

I never, ever remember having an imaginary friend during my childhood as so many spiritually-aware people seem to have done. I feel that, in my own mind, I was always different and don't deny having a very strong imagination – a factor which at that time was perhaps a little too advanced for my family either to understand or appreciate. My school days were another story. Although I did quite well and "got by" at school,

15

those days were not the happiest of times. I really hated woodwork and would try every excuse in the book to avoid it, all of which worked very well until the teacher realised.

I also hated certain sports, especially cricket and football, which I had difficulty in coming to terms with, never having a good sense of kicking the ball in the right direction. I was only ever allowed into the school football team as a last, desperate measure, and was not really popular with other members of it. I don't think I even owned any football boots, but I did enjoy school sports days and usually managed to get picked for the high jump and relay team. Although I never won anything, at least I enjoyed them.

My first job, on leaving school, was in "Wetherill's", the local village store, which had its own bakery. Delivering the bread around the village was my job each morning. I had to ride a three-wheeled bike with a box at the front; it was not easy to ride and had a mind of its own. Although I had difficulty manoeuvring bends and corners, and the bread often ended up in the road, it did get delivered eventually, even if it was often out of shape.

I remained at the store for about a year, but by then I was feeling very restless and realised that the country life was not what I wanted; I needed people around me with whom I could associate more comfortably. I required a challenge in my life and wanted to achieve something different and unusual, although I didn't know what.

Eventually, much to everyone's surprise, I decided that I wanted to work in a hospital and, on applying for a job at the local Newark hospital, I was accepted as a pre-nursing student, being too young, at seventeen, to be eligible for training as a student nurse. There were very few male nurses in 1955, and had never been any in Newark. There was another young man who started at the same time called John; he was planning to be a radiographer and this was to be part of his training. At first we were both treated with a lot of curiosity, some people thinking us as "cissies" to want to be nurses – not that it bothered me what people thought. I was beginning at last to enjoy my new job and changed life-style, being able to relate to the people I was now mixing with in my new situation.

The combined frustrations of growing up, dealing with my emotions and wanting my independence, resulted in my soon feeling that I needed to move further away from my family and existing friends, as I sadly felt that I had outgrown them even though I was at such an early stage of my life.

I applied and was accepted as a student nurse at Markfield Sanatorium in Leicestershire, a situation where I was able to live and work with people I could relate to, who had similar interests to me. This was one of the happy times in my teenage years to which I can still look back with a smile. I made some very special friends and have good memories of the patients during my time there. Now we have all gone our separate ways

16

and I wish I had kept in contact with them.

At that time I heard some surprising news from my parents; there was to be another addition to the family. After a seven-year gap since Jenny's birth, there was to be another sister named Alma.

In 1958, restlessness had again set in and change was calling. I decided to move to London and was accepted by the South-Western Hospital in Stockwell as a student nurse. Unfortunately, after nursing there for only a few months, I received my call-up papers to join the R.A.F. Although the hospital applied for my exemption from service, I still had to go, but they promised my job would be there after my two years' service were completed.

Following basic training in a camp in Bedfordshire, I was posted "up north" to near Lytham St. Annes; the training course I had applied for as a radio operator was refused, but because of my nursing experience, I was drafted into the medical corps. Due to this, my training days were more fun for me than for some of the others, and I was lucky at exam time and had no difficulty in "passing out". I was then posted to a radar unit at Bawdsey in Suffolk where I could not settle. That is one experience I should not like to repeat and was relieved when eventually I was drafted out on medical grounds.

I resumed my career at the South-Western Hospital, where I was very happy and, although I left nursing for a year to work on the London buses which was an enjoyable break, I still longed to continue with my nursing. I joined Grove Park Hospital and Lewisham Hospital and, having finally completed my exams, remained at Grove Park as a staff nurse.

My first spiritual contact occurred at that time, as I met someone who apparently was a medium. I was invited to see them demonstrate at a spiritualist church in Blackheath, but with so many other things happening at that time in my life, it didn't mean much to me and I never followed it up.

My life was becoming more varied. One of the things I had become involved in at the hospital was to encourage another side of my character to emerge – I had taken part in the hospital concerts which had proved quite successful, and this led to my singing in a group formed by Michael Dent, one of the charge nurses. Following singing lessons at the then famous Maurice Berman School, I enjoyed the chance to sing in pubs and clubs, but that was not all. Many of my friends at the time were connected with the world of antiques and a very good friend named John Walsh and I decided to have a go at opening a small antique shop in Lewisham. The shop was stocked mostly with things we had battled for during the previous months at local jumble sales and auction rooms. With so much going on then in my life, I wonder how on earth I had the energy and time to do everything, but in those days life seemed easier and more fun.

During this time when I was involved in three different jobs, I had moved to Joydens Wood Road in Bexley, Kent. I was nursing part-time to enable me to concentrate on the shop a little more, but again my life took another twist. Due to my occasional singing dates, an agency signed me up to do "extra" and "walk-on" parts for TV and commercials. Life was getting much more complicated and changes had to be made. We sold the antique shop and, with John, I took a stall in the famous Chelsea Antiques Market, King's Road. As this progressed, I was able to give up my nursing career for good, which by then I was finding very frustrating. Now, with the stall, I hoped to take my chance and try to make a success of the TV work. Someone must have been looking after me, for most weeks I was busy doing TV work and commercials, even getting the occasional speaking part. This resulted in a lot of photographic work, mostly for foreign magazines, over the next ten years or so.

Once more fate took over. I had reached a difficult phase emotionally and realised I had to reorganise my life once again. The antique trade was becoming more difficult to buy for and, as I was already running it on a shoestring budget, I had to accept that I owed more on the stock than the stall was worth. Finally, Chelsea had to go. At first, I was still able to survive doing occasional TV work and being very glad of the repeat cheques that so often saved the day. I still occasionally did antique fairs at weekends at various venues, but it was a struggle and, in the end, I was even having to sell my personal bits and pieces which I had acquired over the years as security, in order to keep my flat and pay the bills.

One day in September 1984, I came to my senses, knowing that I could no longer live in "cloud-cuckoo land". That is when I made the best decision of my life and returned to Lincolnshire where I was born, as told in my book, *Just a Touch Away*.

As I look back over the past fifty years of my life, I was never really spiritually aware, nor had any impressive spiritual experiences, although they were put before me – I was not meant to relate to them until now. I do know, though, that all the events and happenings in my material and emotional life were important, as now they are very much used to give me strength, to enable me to understand others and to make me sensitive enough to be able to work with spirit.

My family and friends are still surprised in the new me. It is as if they see the old Bryan as a completely different person who has now a definite aim in life to help others.

I hope that sharing my life experiences with you will help others who find life frustrating to understand that we can use all that happens to us, learning from it and finding ways of putting it all to good use in helping others.

Perhaps we may now be able to accept that spirit will always give us the chance to work with them, whatever the conditions of our lives may be, or whatever our age. To me, it is the most natural gift to be able to have and, by being chosen as a voice for spirit, I am honoured to have the opportunity to try to use the gift wisely, not only to spread the word of spirit, but also to help people in many different ways, of whatever race or creed they may be.

With mother (1938) outside cottage.

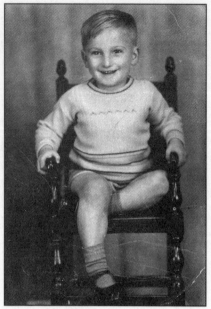

Myself at four years old.

School Photograph – I'm on the back row, last one on the right.

Mrs. Sleaford.

R.A.F. days.

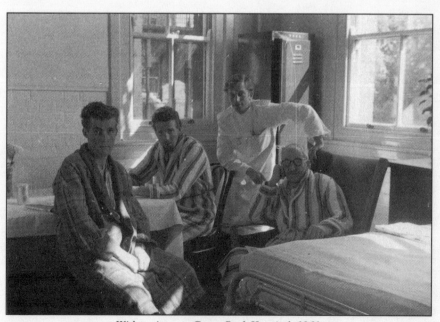

With patients at Grove Park Hospital, 1961.

Receiving prize for best student nurse, 1962.

BRYAN
CRAVEN

Early modelling days.

TV appearance on Norman Wisdom Show, 1973.

Chapter Two

MY SPIRITUAL AWARENESS

May I now take you a little further to show how I was introduced to the wonderful world of spirit? Let me tell you about my introduction to my guides and the joy which followed and show you something of the fun and also the serious side of spirit work.

Until seven years ago, I was leading an average sort of life with its problems, its ups and downs, when it changed like something out of a story book and here I now am writing and working with spirit.

Just before reaching my half-century in life, during the month of May 1986, I was made aware of this special gift – I had been chosen to work for spirit.

It was to be a new beginning for me, not only was my attitude to change, but the peace and happiness missing from so much of my life were also given to me.

In November 1984, I moved from Bexley in Kent to a village previously unknown to me, Kirkby la Thorpe, Lincolnshire, not realising just how much my life was about to change. I arrived there on Bonfire Night, 5th November, to live at 2 Mount Lane Farm. My intentions were to commute backwards and forwards to London with the Antique Fairs, but as this did not work out, I was out on a limb, not knowing anyone locally, and becoming – for the first time in my life – one of the unemployed which I found very hard to accept. Suddenly, my life became very frustrating. All my friends were in London and my nearby family had their own lives to live, but I would visit them as often as possible as they were all within a twenty mile radius, my sister Jenny in Lincoln often having a visit from me.

Trying to make friends was not easy for me at first, as I didn't drink and wasn't interested in the usual places where one goes to meet people. I was a bit sorry for myself.

One day, in response to a casual remark of mine about the problem, someone suggested various places I should try, one being the local spiritualist church at Sleaford. At that time I had not got the courage to venture there on my own and the few people I had started to know, when invited to go with me, responded with "Not me", "It's all that creepy stuff", and were afraid of "the unknown". However, one day a friend called Peter said, out of the blue, "OK, I'll give it a try," so on the following Sunday, although a little apprehensive, I made my first visit to Sleaford Spiritualist Church, a decision which was to completely alter my life.

On entering the church, we were welcomed with a smile and the words, "Hello, nice to see you," which broke down any barriers and enabled me to relax and enjoy the evening. I really felt at home with the church and the people and could not wait for the following Sunday to come around. It became quite an event in my social life. At times I was quite surprised I was always made welcome, because over the weeks I attended and sat at the back, I was not always on my best behaviour. Sometimes things went wrong, like people singing out of tune. I remember one evening when the visiting medium was giving his philosophy in trance and had turned so that he was giving his address to the wall; all we could see was the back of his head. I would often, like then, end up with a fit of the giggles and often got glared at by the older members of the church. I quite expected to be told I was not the sort of person suitable to be one of their members but, to my surprise, I was invited to apply for membership. I began my probation period, and after attending for a few months, was given full membership of the church. I learned later that, among those who did not then know my name, I was referred to as "the giggler".

As a regular member of the church, I began to feel at home living in Sleaford and, as well as making some new friends, I was getting to know a little more about spirit. I was also attending a healing session at Grantham, which was another form of spiritual work where I could sit and discuss things with friends. One day, two ladies I had become friendly with, invited me to go with them to a new church which had just started at Bingham. This proved to be another important step in my spiritual awareness, although I was completely unaware of its significance at the time.

There in Bingham during April 1986, I received my first life-changing message from a medium named Joyce Gearing. When she approached me with messages – including one about somebody in the army – I could not understand what she meant, but as she was about to leave me to talk to someone else in the congregation, she suddenly said, "You are very spiritually aware and should develop." This took me completely by surprise, and after the service, my friends Ann and Yvonne suggested I talk further to the medium. Imagine my surprise when Joyce told me that her home was in Sleaford. When I said that was where I was now living, Joyce promptly gave me her telephone number and invited me to go to talk with her.

On the following Wednesday when I was in town, I bumped into Joyce who remembered me and arranged there and then for me to visit her in her mobile home near the spiritualist church.

Although a little apprehensive by the time Friday came around, I was so excited that I could not wait to get there and turned up a little early. Joyce gave me a lovely welcome and a cup of tea and introduced me to a friend of hers, a gentleman in the R.A.F. at Cranwell whom Joyce was also helping to develop spiritually.

Once I had drunk my tea and relaxed a little, Joyce started to explain to me something about spiritualism and how it worked. She talked of communicating and of guides, which intrigued me. When Joyce asked if I would like to know who my own guides were, I quickly replied, "Yes." Joyce proceeded to place a chair in the centre of the room and asked me to sit in it. She told me to close my eyes and relax, and to place my hands outwards with the palms upwards.

With the help of the R.A.F. gentleman, who stood in front of me giving extra spiritual energy, Joyce began talking me through what I was experiencing. It was like drifting away, no longer being aware of the room I was in and feeling very peaceful. I was aware of feeling as if I was walking in long grass with the sun on my back, smelling the fresh grass around me, and while this was happening, Joyce talked quietly, telling me what she could see. She began to describe an Indian Chief who was with me and asked me what I was now seeing. I was being shown a foot and started to feel that I wanted to run. Joyce confirmed that it was the name of my guide, "Running Foot", and stated that he belonged to the Sioux tribe. Joyce continued to support me as I became increasingly aware of Running Foot and, as this fascinating experience continued, I was told that I would know when Running Foot would be with me as he would make me positively aware of him. He promptly placed his tomahawk in my out-stretched hand and immediately I felt the weight on my hands increasingly until I asked him to take it away. He then placed it back again so that I would be able to relate next time I sat and linked up with him. He continued for a short while enabling me to become aware of different sensations and placing his tomahawk once more in my hands so that I would get used to this new awareness of his presence. The experience was so beautiful that I could feel tears of joy running down my cheeks.

A little later, Joyce began talking to me again, explaining that there was another guide wanting to be accepted and this was my healing guide. Very reluctantly letting go of my union with Running Foot, I relaxed to allow the other guide to link up with us. This time, I found it much more difficult as I was beginning to experience an awful feeling of sadness. When Joyce asked what I could see, all I could describe was the feeling of being swathed in bandages from head to foot, leaving only the eyes visible. These eyes shone bright green, a much brighter colour than I had ever seen.

On relaxing and asking for more information, I became aware of a very young boy who had passed into spirit. I was impressed with the figure eighteen and with the throat trouble which had been the cause of his passing into the spirit world. Joyce prompted me to ask him for his name, which was spelt out for me as "Kuros". He was a Greek Egyptian and the bandages represented a mummy, so now I had another special person to link up with. Joyce brought me reluctantly back to being myself again and made me another cup of tea.

I felt as happy as a sand-boy. I don't think I shall ever be able to put into words my exact feelings at that time, as there are no words to describe such joy. We sat and discussed what had happened and talked about how I was now to take this new-found spiritual awareness a step farther.

Chapter Three

MY AWARENESS OF MY SPIRIT FAMILY

Now I had become aware of my spiritual gift, taking this wonderful awareness a stage further was a process which was about to begin. Joyce advised me to meditate with my new-found friend, Running Foot, and suggested that I try to form a communication with him by sitting at 9.30 p.m. in a quiet room in which I felt comfortable, to see what transpired. I had been unable to understand on my arrival at Mount Lane Farm why I felt so uncomfortable in my bedroom, but now surprisingly decided that this was the correct room in which to have this special union with spirit, and promptly prepared it, placing a comfortable chair in the room ready for my evening session. This was to be the big moment. Would it work? Everything was nice and quiet; there was no radio or television on and I sat in the chair and proceeded to make my first attempt at linking with spirit through my guide, Running Foot.

I made myself comfortable, closed my eyes and placed my hands on my knees with the palms upwards. I then tentatively asked my guide, Running Foot, to join me. Within a few seconds I was aware of heavy pressure on my hands. This was Running Foot's tomahawk being placed there as his proof that he was with me. At the same time I could feel myself becoming very relaxed and sensed a warm feeling all around me, which lasted for a few minutes. Then I suddenly became aware in my mind of a pair of eyes, so I asked Running Foot whether he wanted me to see. At this, my head was made to nod, which I understood to mean "Yes". Then it all happened. Suddenly, pictures were flashing before me; it was just like looking at a television set. Some made sense, others I could not really relate to, and this continued for what seemed to be ages. In reality it only lasted for between fifteen and twenty minutes. Then everything went blank and the warmth and pressure around began to wane slowly. I wanted to open my eyes which by now felt as if I had been crying, but that moment was one of pure joy and happiness. I thanked Running Foot for allowing this special evening to happen and assured him that I would be there again the next night at the same time.

27

I arrived downstairs still trying to remember what I had seen and experienced and wrote everything down on a note-pad.

The following night could not come soon enough for me and once again I proceeded in the same opening ritual, asking to be united with Running Foot. This time, the first impression I received was a picture of an ear. On asking if this meant that I was to listen, my head again was moved with a nod. Then my next lesson began. This time I was made aware of many different sounds, from the rush of a waterfall to wind blowing the trees; I heard different animals and music and also voices which were very muffled and not really clear. Once more, this continued for nearly half an hour, and after thanking Running Foot, I wrote down the experiences I could remember. By now, it was becoming very difficult to wait until the time for my next communication with Running Foot and the excitement was hard to contain.

The third night had now arrived. I wondered what learning would be in store and I was not to be disappointed, for again I was very quickly into my union with Running Foot. This time when I closed my eyes, the first impression I was shown was of two hands joined together. At first I did not understand this and then the picture changed to a belt being fastened, followed by ears and eyes. Then it clicked. I realised that the pictures from the first night and the sounds from the previous night would be joined together.

When it all began, it was fascinating working everything out, and before I realised it, my half-hour with Running Foot had passed and it was time to close for the night. I thanked Running Foot for his patience and help and again added what I could remember to the notes of the previous nights.

The fourth night was also about the joining of the pictures and sounds and I wondered whether this was all that would be shown or whether there was more to come.

On the fifth night, Running Foot had an even bigger surprise for me however. As usual, the opening ritual took place and I was awaiting my picture. Instead, I was aware of my head being pulled right back and of wanting to clear my throat. After a few attempts which got me nowhere, I began to feel relaxed; once again, my head went back and this time the sudden burst of very deep laughter filled the room followed by his deep voice saying, "Welcome" and more laughter. It was so loud and powerful that I was actually trembling with emotion and then it was gone. Now I realised that, not only was I able to see and hear things, I was also capable of allowing Running Foot to use me as a channel for his voice. The whole week had produced one special surprise after another and boy, was I in another world. I thought I would never feel ordinary again, but I had to come down to this reality and sort it all out into its correct perspective. Through all that had happened during the week, I had not felt afraid nor questioned it. Everything seemed as natural as learning a new job.

Understandably, by now I was very excited and wanting to tell everyone of my new-found link with spirit. However, I was aware that the few people I knew would avoid me like the plague if they found out, or would consider that I should be committed to the nearest mental hospital, which was just a couple of miles away. The only person I knew who would understand was Joyce, so I phoned to tell her all that had happened. I think that even she thought I was getting carried away and sounded dubious about my claims but invited me over the next week, saying, "We will see."

By now I was eager to experiment much more with my wonderful link with Running Foot and spirit. Now he was teaching me his native songs and I would be happily chanting away whilst in the bath and doing things around the house. It was a good thing I lived on my own and had no neighbours to bother me – I am sure I would have scared them away. Very often during the day, Running Foot would decide it was also time for me to learn some traditional dances to accompany the songs I had been taught. There I would be in my own little world, chanting and dancing with my eyes closed, oblivious to the world and frequently finding myself facing the opposite direction to that in which I had begun. Through all of this, I never knocked into anything nor injured myself. All of this was great for me, but once again it was very frustrating not to be able to show it off.

When it was time for my visit to Joyce, she greeted me and said, "Right, let's see if what you say is really spirit." She proceeded to ask me questions and then asked me to link up with Running Foot so that she could question him also. When Joyce had completed everything, she said, "Well, it's definitely spirit. I don't understand how it has happened so quickly without development or help." Spirit obviously knew I was a correct channel for them and I was ready to help with their work from spirit. Joyce said that next time she had a circle, she would like me to sit in and watch what went on. I did attend for a few weeks in the circle but was not really allowed to give my true experience of spirit and was rather resented by one or two people there, who could not accept I should be so spiritually aware in that short space of time when they had sat in many circles and were still trying to succeed in working with spirit. However, it was an experience, but since then I have never become involved in such work.

Now I was more confident of my gift and wanted to spread the word and show people what I could do. I had also been attending a healing group in a hall in Oxford Street, Grantham, and they had decided to have an awareness hour. We would all sit there and then be asked if we had any messages for anyone in the group. Until then I had never really opened up about anything, so people were amazed when I related to a lady there and passed on a message which she understood. That was it. I opened up and told them all that had happened to me and how I was now able to link with spirit. The next few weeks were great fun and more people were coming because those that were there had talked about me. Once the news started spreading, people would invite me to their homes and I would give them a sitting. As I was at that time unemployed, someone suggested that since I could not accept money, they would bring me a few groceries such as tea, coffee or even cat food. I never had to buy tea or sugar, etc. for the following three years. Even my family benefited from the excess of food.

As my spirit gift progressed, more people wanted sittings and I was working whenever I could. By now, I had to sort out what spirit wanted me to do, not using it to tell people's future, but to help those who had lost loved ones, giving evidence that those who had passed were now at peace and relaying guidance to encourage them on their correct pathway.

People at my local spiritualist church who knew of my gift tried to advise me. Others would knock me and tell me that I would never be allowed on a platform or permitted to give a service until I had been in the movement for at least three years, until I had joined the S.N.U and been accepted by them, and so on. I thought I should have to wait and, in the meantime, get on with what I was already doing.

Three months into this period, I received a phone call out of the blue from Les Hamp of Sleaford Spiritualist Church. They had had a cancellation and asked if I would like to take the service the following Sunday. Without thinking, I said yes. On putting down the phone, my doubts appeared. What had I agreed to do? On asking spirit, however, they said it would be O.K.

The week passed and I never felt anxious or thought much about the Sunday and what would happen. Sunday came. This was my first real test. I had to get up there and show everyone what I could do and prove to those who doubted that my spirit communication was real.

On arriving at the church, it was as if I was there but felt very different, like I was looking at myself and doing something that was being controlled by a different me. It is hard to explain how I actually felt, but it was definitely spirit in control. The service started and, when it came to the address, I just closed my eyes and let spirit come through to give the talk. Although I thought I sounded nervous, everyone said it came over positively and clearly, and then the clairvoyant demonstration came and went smoothly, with information being accepted by the recipients of the messages. Soon it was time for the closing prayer and the service came to an end. The ordeal had come and gone much more smoothly than I could have hoped for. Now I knew that I was capable of working for spirit both in public and in private, reaching out to people and telling them of spirit and its special link with us here on the earth plane.

Since this very quick awakening to my link with spirit, my work has progressed as you will see from this book. I hope that my story will encourage many more of you to go forward spiritually, whatever obstacles are put before you.

Chapter Four

RUNNING FOOT

I know that some people think that mediums put too much emphasis on our guides. I am certain, however, that I should not have had such confidence to work with spirit as I do, without my lovely link with my guide, Running Foot. Knowing him and the other members of my spiritual family gives me strength to do my work.

Their guidance is always available to me and, when I am working with other people's families and friends in spirit, they always help me to overcome any difficulties I experience. If the messages are not clear, or I have difficulty understanding the spirit communicator, they always come to my aid. I have often sent out an S.O.S. to them for help during a sitting, for extra help and strength of different kinds. Sometimes I need a more positive link with the spirit voice or have a situation which has been given symbolically and I cannot find a suitable interpretation for it. That is when Running Foot and my spirit family come particularly to help, giving me whatever is needed, clarity, patience or more understanding.

Running Foot has become an extension of me – like a father, brother and friend all rolled into one. He is so important to me that he is always mentioned. I explain to people who he is, why he is with me and how we work together. He is talked about at demonstrations and church services and introduced to my many sitters, who are not only interested by his work but also enjoy the fun which at times he brings into my life.

Some mediums are reluctant to tell people who their guide is, but I always give the information when I am asked. It is surprising how many people are interested and want information about guides, sometimes referring to them as "guardian angels". If spirit will give me their guide, I try to relate as much as possible about the guide, as to their origin, name and the work they hope to do. I try not to give out information about spirit guides during public demonstrations, as this is not the place to go into detail, and therefore the message would be wasted. Very rarely, when giving a service where everyone is spiritually aware and hoping to develop, I will relate to a guide and give information relevant to that person. Sadly, I have been at services as a member of the congregation, where the serving medium has given everyone receiving a message a guide as well, sometimes bombarding them with details of several guides at the same time, to the amusement of those present who know little of spirit work. To me, this way of working suggests a lack of ability to pass on positive messages and a means of trying to hide the fact.

I feel that the guides and helpers are there to help us to understand, to join the spirit world and the material world together in love and harmony, and to help our loved ones communicate with us.

Many mediums work with several guides or helpers. Some of the guides are with that medium to strengthen their knowledge and to learn how to communicate; when the time is right, they will be allocated as a special guide or door-keeper of a person on earth. A door-keeper is a guide who protects and guards the medium, trying to control spirit communication and deciding which spirit communicator gains access to the medium.

A frequently asked question is why so many guides appear to be Red Indians, Chinese, Egyptians, nuns or monks, and if I have time I always try to answer this. If we look back over past generations, especially of tribal races, we see that their belief systems included spirit being able to communicate through thought and meditation; their loved ones were taken to burial grounds together with their possessions and special gifts from their families to commence their journey into the next world. When we look back over past generations within our own society, we see there spirit being frowned upon, it was considered taboo, evil to believe in spirit communication; people who did believe such things or practice working with spirit were classed as indulging in witchcraft and were tortured, burned and drowned. Spirit communication was therefore very effectively restricted. This is why races from other parts of the world are better able to help us, choosing to continue to link with this earth plane. To do so has always been part of their culture and belief and holds no threat; it is the way life always has been for them and the way they expect it to be.

Thank goodness, the negative attitudes in our society are now changing. Spiritualism is becoming more and more talked about. The misunderstood aspects of different forms of spirit work are being explained so that people no longer consider it so mysterious and weird. They are shown how it works, and healing, in particular, helps many people. The questions of today's younger generation regarding spiritualism are no longer met with vague answers. They are interested in truth, and judge for themselves what to believe. The days are gone when people are dictated to about what they may believe, although sad to say, there are still, and no doubt always will be, those dear souls who cannot believe there is any other valid creed than their own. These people continue to condemn spiritualism as the work of the devil and try to force us into believing that only they have the answers and know who may and who may not enter heaven. They teach that if you do not accept their teaching, you are not a Christian and must be evil.

When we all leave this earth plane, we shall all be made welcome in the spirit world, treated as equals and given the same chance to be at peace. If we wish to come back to talk to our loved ones, it is allowed, whatever we may have believed in whilst here on earth.

I hope that by explaining about our guides and special helpers in the spirit world, you see that they are not imaginary figures nor just an image we use to impress people; they are real people who, like us, lived on the earth and have now moved on to a higher plane – their second home – and wish to join and work with us to bring peace, love and understanding. They are not here to interfere in our lives or try to lead our lives for us; we are the ones responsible for doing that and for creating the pattern of our own life experience.

Now you can see that my spirit family are very special to me – not only for the help they give me, but for the trust they have in me to work spiritually for them. All of them are special in their different ways, but most of all Kuros, my healing friend, and, of course, the one I often refer to as "The Boss", Running Foot, which makes him laugh. I suppose I am a little more fanatical about relating to Running Foot, especially talking about him and showing him off, not hiding him away as some strange person I slink off to talk to for help and guidance. In my home, there is a very special painting of him which takes pride of place over everything else. The painting was created at the very beginning of my spiritual awareness by a talented local artist, Sheila Parkinson, who to begin with was, I think, rather unsure about doing it.

A few weeks after I first became aware of Running Foot, I felt the need to have an image of him, and that day I was sitting in a cafe, having a cup of tea with Sheila, when I asked if she would do the painting for me. Taking out a piece of paper, she promptly began to make notes and said to leave it with her and she would make a rough drawing to see if that was what I wanted. A few weeks later, in the same cafe, Sheila produced a sketch of Running Foot, and he quickly got me to change the shape of his nose and eyes and went on to mention the colours of his head-dress, making great emphasis on the colour of the wooden beads around his neck. Now this was ready for Sheila to go ahead and put together.

A while later, I had a call from Sheila saying the painting was ready and would I like to go and see it. I honestly cannot describe how I felt on seeing the painting. I could feel tears of happiness in my eyes, yet I was surprised, as I was expecting Running Foot to appear as an old man, as I had seen him. When I asked him why he looked younger, his reply was that he wanted to be shown as he was at the same age I was, which to me was very special and made our bond much closer. Sheila said that when it came to colouring him, it was as if she had been taken over. It all flowed so easily and it was as if he himself were in charge. The picture is admired by everyone because of its changes of expression and the life which radiates from it.

Most people will know that Running Foot is on the cover of my books because, without him, there would be no books. There is a story in my book, *I'm Here Listening*, about how I had a tattoo made of him on both my forearms and, more recently he has put in an appearance for everyone, as I have had a painting of him done on the bonnet of my car. It certainly causes a few heads to turn and is a good conversation piece, especially in London; a few people have tried to make fun by standing in front of the car, putting up their hand and saying, "How" which at least means he is getting recognition.

Running Foot and I have a regular routine when we give a demonstration or church service, so that I know he is with me. Just before the clairvoyance, I ask him if he is ready to join me. At that time, I feel his head-dress being placed on my head and he gives a quick shake of the feathers. Then we are both in harmony and ready to work spiritually. At the end of each evening, I thank not only Running Foot, but the rest of my spirit family for all their work and help and, often as I am driving home, we have a conversation about the evening and look for ways to improve the presentation. If I have made any errors, Running Foot will show me why and give me guidance. Sometimes, if I have felt a little flat following a service, he will try to reassure me and raise my thoughts. However, Running Foot and my spirit family never tell me that I have to do as they say; they give me advice to digest and use to the best of my ability. At the end of the day, it is down to me; the decisions are mine. Out of all this, though, the lovely thing is that we all trust each other and that is why we can work in love, truth and harmony.

Myself with painting of Running Foot on the car.

Picture (1986) with painting of Running Foot by Sheila Parkinson, local artist.

Chapter Five

A MESSAGE FROM RUNNING FOOT

This chapter was inspired by my spirit/friend/guide – Running Foot. In the month of February, 1987, at about eleven o'clock one evening, I was made aware of Running Foot and the urge to do some recording on tape. Although not really sure of what he had in mind, I proceeded to set up the tape-recorder and waited to see what would happen. After a very short period of meditation, I was aware of Running Foot's voice wanting to come through and talk, and so closing my eyes and relaxing, I started the tape running. With no more ado, Running Foot started to talk and talk. This went on for nearly half-an-hour until, finally, he bade me "Goodnight" and I was able to play back the tape to find out what had been said.

The following transcript is exactly as recorded, word-for-word, on the tape. This was to be the first tape of several, as over the next months, another four messages were also recorded, each one produced late at night when everywhere was peaceful with no outside or inside noise. I still have these tapes but have made copies of the recordings for friends and other people who could benefit from Running Foot's words.

Since the last tape in 1988, I have often asked him if there would be any more, but so far there have been none. The answer I receive whenever I ask is that, now we have a closer understanding, it is not necessary for him to dictate on to tape as our understanding of each other is in such a close and special bond that our thoughts are one, and Running Foot does not need to use our modern technology to get his words over to me.

Transcript of tape by Running Foot, February 1987
Oh, my friend, it is so nice to be able to come down once more to link with you. We are so pleased when we are allowed this moment to tell you a little of ourselves and of our work within the world of spirit.

It is such a pleasant and happy union when we are allowed to communicate not only through the body of a person on the material plane, but also allowed to talk in one's voice after many years of silence.

We hope we can come down many times to tell you what we see and what we hope you will want to hear from the world of spirit.

You see, my friend, when one leaves the material plane, it is only one's body that is left behind. Although there is sadness for the people who remain here, there is much joy and happiness for the person who has come to join us in the world of spirit.

Most times, nearly every time – I will correct myself – they are met by their loved ones – by people already here in the world of spirit. So, my friends, they are not alone; they do not feel bewildered or lost. They can link up and they can join up with the people who left them many years before.

Many people when they reach the world of spirit are given the chance to help, to link up and join once again with the material plane. But many, my friends, decide that they would prefer to stay in the state of peace to which they have woken. But, my friends, they always wish to link up with their loved ones, given the opportunity, as when you come to talk with us. Sometimes it is not possible at a certain time for a person to communicate with you; sometimes they are unable to link with the person you have come to see, so do not give up when the conditions are bad, you will once again receive the happy union.

Many of you are very surprised when they come back, that they are able to tell you so many things about themselves, not only the way they passed, but also things that mean a great deal to you but nothing to many other people, because you see, my friend, not only do they take their love with them, their memories and their thoughts of you are with them always. Although you may think, once they have left you, they are not aware of what is going on, they are able to have glimpses of your life as it progresses. They see the new children which are born into the family which they were not here to be able to rejoice with, but they do rejoice with you in spirit. They watch that child. As those children progress, they try to help them; they try to guide them. They also try to guide you to show you a pathway. Many, many times you will feel the presence of your loved ones and, many times, you will say, "It is my imagination." Oh, no, my friends – it is your loved ones trying to communicate in the only way they know how; sometimes it is by a brief touch, sometimes it is in association with a memory, sometimes one is very lucky and able to have a glimpse of your loved one. This, my friend, is sometimes difficult because many times it is inclined to make you a little wary, but they mean you no harm. It is that strong love bond which they wish to communicate with you. They wish to say, "Good-bye" and let you know they are safe and happy with us.

It is also like, my friends, when a young one – a child – is taken away from you at a very early age, when it has not been given the chance to be born into the world. These children are given a chance to grow; they prosper; they become the children of the spirit world and they learn, and at a later date in time are given a chance on the material plane. So you see, my friend, when a child is lost at a very early age, they are not really lost – it is only that you cannot see them. You cannot touch them, but they are still your children and they will be here when you come to link up with us.

Also, my friends, there are many other ways of people who pass into the world of spirit. Some, unfortunately, are taken not by means which you call "accident" or "fate"; these people too are given a chance to progress; they do not stop to grow. They prosper and they too will be given another chance to live again. Even those that unfortunately take their own lives by their own hands are given the choice too, because, my friends, it is not always a crime. It is the person – the imbalance within that person – which causes it to happen and many, many times, my friend, they do not mean to leave you behind but unfortunately it is too late for them to call themselves back; sometimes they are lucky, but sometimes it is meant to be.

We try to show you glimpses of the person here with us in the world of spirit. Each one of us has a chance once we are here; we have a choice to grow spiritually, to learn, to be of use or, my friends, you have that choice of remaining at peace with yourself. You are not forced into any situation; as you have on the material plane, you also continue with the freedom of choice. But people say when you have left this earth, there is no further life. May I reassure each and every one of you there is a lot to look forward to; there is another life here to look forward to, not only linking up with the people you once knew, but to wait for your loved ones to link up with and eventually join you in the spirit world.

You can go on for an indefinite time and progress and become more knowledgeable like myself, put the knowledge to great use by being able to come down and talk with you and tell you a little of our work. This, today, is a very, very minor part of the work we do. We look down at each and every one of you and hope that we can show there is only joy, happiness and laughter in the life hereafter.

We look forward once more to talking with you at a later date. I thank each and every one of you for allowing me to come down and talk with you and tell you a little of my work in the world of spirit. May God bless each and every one of you and, until we talk once again, my friends, may I bid you, "Good day".

Running Foot
Sioux Chief
February 1987.

MANKIN – BUDDHIST MONK
LEADER + PHILOSOPHER

KUROS – GREEK EGYPTIAN
1300 BC
HEALER + UNDERSTANDING

MASSUED – EGYPT
RELIGIOUS TEACHINGS

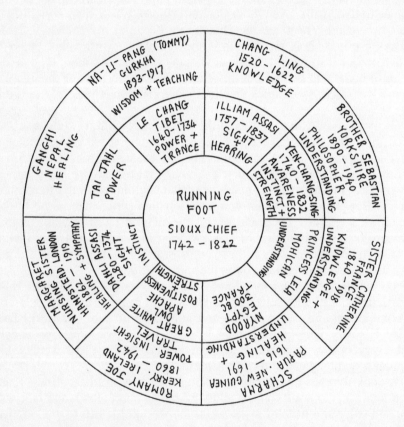

This diagram shows the special people who I call my 'Spiritual Family'. As most of you are now aware, Running Foot is my main guide, otherwise known as "The Boss". Kuros is my healing guide, and is very special to me, and Mankin is the one I turn to when Running Foot runs out of answers for some of my questions.

The others, as you will read, have their own special qualities to offer as part of my work, and we are all there to help and learn from each other. Eventually, when they have learned more about communication and spiritual matters, they will be given the opportunity to work with another medium on a much closer link, and will become someone else's 'Main Guide'.

EVEN AS THE WIND BLOWS

Even as the wind blows
Sending life in all directions,
Even as the rain falls
Like the shedding of your tears,
Even as the sun shines on the earth
And on the many spheres which shine
Yet brighter,
Life goes on.
In that fleeting moment
When the butterfly emerges from its
Chrysalis, know this . . .
All life is forever.
And as the soul reaches its journey's end here,
So it transmutes . . .
To become yet closer to God.

JOHN BRETT

Chapter Six

LEARNING THE HARD WAY

The way is not always easy. During my short time as a working medium I have come up against many different situations, and in many of them, I have had to learn the hard way about people's attitudes to me and their expectations towards my spiritual gift.

Many people have strange attitudes to mediumship and see me accordingly. At the beginning of the time I learned to link up with spirit, I had few friends around, having left most of my own friends in Kent and the people I was in contact with locally were mostly acquaintances. However, suddenly I acquired a great number of "friends" who would invite me to their homes or parties, and although I was not wholly aware of the reason, it soon became clear. Since at that time I was unemployed and without a great deal to do, I did not mind being encouraged to demonstrate my gift continually whenever I called for a cup of tea or went to a party. Friends and neighbours who had been told about my gift would appear as if from nowhere and be invited in to talk to me. Naturally I was flattered by all this attention. Sometimes there would be as many as eight people in the room and I would be showing off my links with spirit, naturally all of them wanted a free message. It was good entertainment and I was the star attraction, but soon the penny began to drop that it was my gift not my friendship which was the attraction. Nonetheless, it was good training and enabled me to progress more quickly with my development spiritually and also I was now becoming known for my mediumistic work.

I began to limit these situations, looking for other directions in which to improve and strengthen my spirit gift, still continuing to visit those who I felt regarded me as a friend as well as a medium, but even then, with some it became progressively difficult.

Sometimes, as soon as I had been offered a cup of tea, people would sit there with pen and paper at the ready, just waiting for me to give them messages and mostly wanting to know about the future. I explained to them that I didn't feel I could help them much more, as that was not really what my gift was for and, sadly, that friendship began to wane and invitations became fewer. In all this, however, spirit was teaching me to understand the attitudes of people and their reasoning.

Another important aspect of my learning at that stage of my spiritual progress was the advice of people who were very spiritually aware as a result of years of experience, who wished to help me. Much of it was totally genuine and I was grateful to receive it but not, I am afraid, all of it. There were some who appeared somewhat envious who seemed intent on kerbing my enthusiasm by telling me to slow down, saying I was going too fast and that my days of being allowed to work as a platform medium were still years away. Thank goodness, their negative talk did not affect me, as I concentrated on listening to my great friend and guide Running Foot and on my expanding spiritual family. Within three months of my spiritual awakening, I was invited to take that memorable first service at an S.N.U. church, so I was glad that I had not been intimidated, for spirit knew I was capable of doing their work even with such limited experience.

I realise how frustrating it must be for those who have faithfully tried for years to achieve their spiritual goal by sitting in circles, when someone like me comes along without previous spiritual awareness or any basic training, and gets up and gives a service, but spirit will always use those who can spread their message, whoever they may be.

Another very enlightening episode was meeting another medium through the church. My first impression of this person was that he seemed genuine and knowledgeable and wanted to help me, offering to show me all there was to know about working with spirit and developing my knowledge of spiritual teachings. I was eager to listen to anything which would help me progress but soon learned that things are not always what they seem. This person was very much into the dramatic side of spiritualism and had obviously dabbled in the dark side of spirit. Although I was hesitant about linking with this person, my mind was telling me that I could not comment on what I knew nothing about. Running Foot assured me I would come to no harm as I was too strong and spirit would help me, so for the next few weeks I attended this person's home whilst keeping my own counsel. I was told I was to be shown the wonder of spirit – how to make objects move at a glance, how to control people by thought, etc., but to be honest nothing ever occurred or materialised as promised. I never witnessed anything moving about the house or any other strange physical phenomena. However, having heard the way this person talked, I can understand weak or vulnerable people being frightened and manipulated. At the time I was very raw and not knowledgeable enough to attempt to say much. I was getting concerned though, in spite of Running Foot's assurances that I would not be harmed, about what this person's intentions were and the direction I was being led in. I need not have worried; Spirit had it all in hand, but it was valuable experience for any such situations which might arise in the future.

Whenever I visited this house after this, as soon as I went in and sat down, I became very sleepy. I had a dreadful job in keeping my eyes open, but as soon as I left, I was wide awake and full of life. As I learned later, this was spirit's way of shutting me off from any influences which were not helpful to me spiritually. Since then there have been other occasions when I have been in an environment which was not in my best interests where spirit wanted me to have nothing to do with those around me and a similar thing has happened.

I was one of the lucky ones in not being influenced by this so-called medium; I had had the sad task of putting right a lot of this person's wrongs. I have had people come to see me with fears of what this person has told them will happen in their lives, expecting dreadful things and deaths if they did not do as they had been told. Many people have come to me in tears afraid of this person's suggested power over them.

I have had many running battles over this situation and shall continue to speak out to try to prevent anyone such as this getting work or being in a position where they can easily prey on those not as spiritually aware as ourselves.

Unfortunately, however, anyone can set themselves up as a medium and advertise. Unless the sitter complains to the police, nothing can be done, but if it is, the media picks it up and once again a bad light is cast over spiritualism.

No doubt as we go through life we all clash with some people; we cannot be liked by everybody. Even as spiritually-aware people, trying to see all sides of someone and why they choose to present themselves as they do, it is still very difficult to want even to reason with such a person.

I have very happy, harmonious relations with most churches where I have been invited to serve as a medium and have come across very little bias, but a church I visited early on in my development still stands out in my memory with regard to the attitude of those supposedly spiritual people in power there.

During the very first year of my mediumship, I had been booked to take the Sunday service in a church I had served before and I was looking forward to my visit. It was a very warm summer's day and I had dressed accordingly – neat and tidy with an open-neck shirt. On arrival, I was warmly welcomed and informed that the chairperson was a member of the District Council and they would chair for me. In introducing myself to the chairperson, I mentioned how I had come suddenly into spiritualism. I was promptly put in my place and notified of the speaker's status in the movement and caustically rebuked for the fact that I was not wearing a suit or tie. When commenting that I could not work feeling uncomfortable and prefer to be casually dressed, the reply I received was, "Well, you must be the Alex Higgins of spiritualism then." I smiled. It was certainly obvious I was disapproved of. The chairperson was evidently not impressed that I had not been trained, nor belonged to the S.N.U.

The service got underway and the address went well and it was time for the clairvoyance. Things were still going smoothly until one lady got a message from her father when, before I had realised what I had said, I repeated the naughty word – "bugger" – which made everyone laugh. When I apologised, the lady said, "That's just what Dad would say," and no more was said, the messages continuing until the end of the clairvoyance. The chairperson very curtly thanked me, and following the closing prayer, I turned to thank the committee. They rudely glared at me and walked off, not saying a word, and completely ignoring me. By this time, my back was up and I remarked to one of the committee on the attitude the person had displayed. The reply was, "You should have seen their face when you let slip that swear-word. If looks could kill, you would be dead by now." I said, "Well, if that's the church's attitude, then I would prefer not to be asked to serve any more." (Although I was asked several times, I stuck to what I said and waited two years before I would accept another booking, and I am pleased to say that I now serve the church on a regular basis.) Since this incident, the person involved has never had a good word to say about me, even telling my own church that I was a charlatan and did not work spiritually but psychically. I know also that this person has tried to block me from getting bookings in the churches where they have influence, but without much success as I still serve the churches within that District Council.

Situations such as this are sad. I know that this person is a very good medium and means well, standing on their beliefs and teachings, but most of it comes from books and not directly from the heart which results in people like them seeming to talk down to others instead of relating to them. I really cannot understand their attitude to me but I do respect them as strong workers for spirit; although they appear to have a dislike for me and my spirit work.

I find it difficult sometimes to explain my certainty that through spirit, we are both working for the same reasons – to help others, to pass spirits' love to those who need that love, and to encourage those who want to become a worker for spirit in whatever pathway they wish to follow.

Chapter Seven

GUIDELINES

Following on the thoughts of the previous chapter, it is obvious that most mediums have their own ways of working, presenting in their own individual ways their awareness of spirit. Whether at a spiritualist church or a public demonstration, most mediums will present their awareness to the best of their ability, but differently one from the other. Many, however, are of the standard school of mediumship, by which I mean those mediums who have been trained to work on the platform. Most are trained by a well-established and learned medium; some develop from being in a circle and are encouraged to channel their spiritual awareness on a wider basis.

These mediums are often of a very high standard, not being allowed on the platform until judged capable of working and relating spiritually, but are often restricted to a set way of working such as has been taught by their tutor. Being afraid to wander from this way of working, they often present messages from spirit communicators without the warmth and personality of the spirit person, or their way of talking whilst on the earth plane. This often results in hesitation about accepting the message because it is not presented in words which the departed person would use.

Naturally, the medium hesitates to allow the real words to be expressed because as well as keeping within the guidelines they have been taught, they are afraid of upsetting those in authority, such as church presidents and committees, and not being booked again. Therefore, messages relayed often appear very basic and impersonal to the recipient, leaving doubt as to whether the message is from the spirit communicator or the medium.

Nowadays there seem to be many more natural mediums being given the chance to work for spirit, such as myself, who have not been told how to use our gift. All the opportunities have been placed before us and before we know it, we are out on the platform working with spirit, learning the hard way about things, learning how to present spirit naturally and adjusting so that we learn from our errors. Spirit obviously knew that by allowing us to have this special gift, we as chosen mediums would represent spirit in the way they wished to be shown, as an extension of life – from our second home, "Spirit".

Many of these mediums who have developed naturally and quickly allow their messages from spirit to be relayed freely and naturally, in the way the communicator wishes to be shown, very often bringing lots of laughter into the churches. Sadly, however, there still remain a number of spiritual people and churches who cannot accept any new ideas and will not even consider mediums who have not been trained through a certified church or the S.N.U. or who have been trained to conform to their committee's approval. If you are unable to conform to their guidelines, you are not welcome or booked to serve their church, even though they have never seen you work, but having heard of your reputation know you will not toe the line.

I am sure I am not alone among mediums in having had the misfortune to occasionally get carried away with the message, and allow the odd naughty word to escape, to the amusement of those listening. Unfortunately some members of the church and particularly the president and higher officials frown on such errors and are quick to condemn instead of realising that nothing is perfect and mistakes are sometimes made. I do accept that it is perhaps not the correct thing to happen in a church and we should be in control of our messages from spirit, but often when working with a very strong spirit communicator, you can be so immersed in translating their message that before you know it, you have passed on the little naughty words they have used as well.

Where I have made genuine mistakes they have not worried me too much but I have learned to be more careful while serving churches and now find that when I have a spirit communicator who would have used such colourful language, I can interpret it in such a way that no one is offended. The recipient of the message knows exactly what the person means because I will inform them of my spirit communicator's character and say that I had better watch what I say and talk more slowly, much to everyone's delight. I know some, however, are sitting there just waiting for me to make that fatal slip up, so when such a message comes through, I usually say that my spirit friend says, "It's a load of rubbish." I carefully say, "Those are my words. My spirit friend describes it much more strongly, but knows I'm not allowed to swear." They know you understand what they mean and usually the recipient of the message will say, "That's them, we knew they would try," and most people in the congregation will laugh along with them, so everyone is pleased with the message and no one should be offended.

Through my problems in this respect, I have been able to correct my mediumship and hopefully strengthen my presentation of spirit, but it has taught me a lot about people who think they have the only answers and must be obeyed, having control over what one can and cannot say.

Mediums like myself – and they are many – will not bow to dictatorship but seek to progress, to express spirit and spirit's work to all who seek it. We shall remain as independent mediums taking our gift and willing to work in any church or similar situation so that all who wish to see us can benefit from the messages we can pass on from our friends in spirit.

These people are just as important as those who consider themselves superior because of earthly qualifications.

As a medium, I hope that I will continue to work for spirit to the best of my ability, spreading spirit's voice to those who need to hear it, showing them that life continues after death. Our spirit family are still part of our lives. They watch over us, guide us, and are always around to support us and keep us on the correct pathway to love and peace.

Chapter Eight

WHAT AM I?

Over the past few years as my work as a medium has progressed, I have had to smile many times at how people refer to me and my work, not just at the image they seem to have of me but also at what they expect me to be able to do.

Very often when people phone me, it is because they have been given my number by someone else and know of me but not actually what I do. Their first words are, "I'm not sure whether I've got the right number, but are you the person who talks to the dead?" or "Are you the gentleman who tells people things?" Some even ask if I read palms or tea-leaves.

When I explain to them about how I work and relate to their family, or friends in spirit, and tell them what they may hopefully receive from a sitting, some reply, "That's what I really want," while others politely say, "Thank you. I will think about it," and you know that they really only want to have their fortunes told, and this is something I definitely do not do.

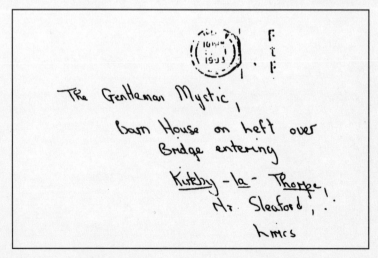

Many also try to contact me by post and I have had some very strange descriptions on the envelopes. When they arrive at the sorting office they must give the staff a laugh and cause the odd joke, but thanks to the important people who do the work at the Post Office, they make sure that each letter arrives at my door.

Chapter Nine

MEDIUMS AND MESSAGES

Even today, it surprises me how many people are still in the dark about how a medium works and as to how spirit communicates with us in our material life.

Many people never think about mediums, nor visit them, until they lose someone close to them and then begin to search. Those who come to see me for the first time say how nervous they feel, saying that going to a local fair and seeing a fortune-teller may be fun, but that seeing a medium is different. Most of those who come for a sitting wish to have communication with their loved ones; some come because they need spiritual guidance – either with something they are hoping to do or perhaps with a family matter that others cannot help them with because they are too close to the situation. A few will come to see a medium because they are just curious and feel they should find out what goes on for themselves. Then there are the odd one or two who come along to try to prove that there is no such thing as spirit communication. After experiencing a sitting, many express surprise that it was not at all what they expected – no strange things happening, no darkened room with candles flickering and incense burning, nor a group of people sitting around a table with hands touching saying, "Is there anybody there?" I suppose this is a classical image of spiritualism portrayed over the years by books, films and television, but things are no longer like "the old days" although seances are still held. Many express their disappointment that it is not that way still, finding it hard to accept that they can have spiritual communication by just sitting with a medium, without certain aids.

There are many ways of communicating with spirit and different mediums work in various ways.

Mediums are those who allow their body to be used as a channel for spirit and are either mental mediums or physical mediums. Quite a number of spiritually-aware people work psychically rather than mediumistically and are known as "psychics", although many people call

51

them mediums also.

I hope I can explain some of the differences. Obviously, some ways in which spirit work are part of my personal experience and those I can be positive about. As to other means of spirit communication, I shall explain only from what I know, and for these, people will have to read up about the subject from those much more knowledgeable than myself, since I have a lot of climbing to do on the spiritual ladder and it may be a long time before I can speak about all the different forms of communication from personal experience.

In the very early stages of my spiritual development, naturally I was very keen to try every form of spirit communication. I experimented for myself, and by doing so, was able to discover the best way for me personally to link with spirit to help those who come to see me.

One common way of working spiritually and relating to a sitter is to hold an item belonging to the person, such as a piece of jewellery, and linking in through this means. This is called "psychometry". For this, the person having the sitting is encouraged to bring with them an object belonging to the one in spirit whom they wish to contact. For some mediums, this is the only way they work, for others it is just a link to concentrate on which is useful but not vital. Many mediums use psychometry in conjunction with their spirit communicator and find it gives them more confidence.

This method can lead to complications. Firstly, it should be explained that the item of jewellery should be something that has been worn only by the one person and not used by different people. Nowadays lots of people buy second-hand jewellery, and if this is the case, the medium giving off information related to the article will probably be giving you lots of information you cannot understand, as it can relate to the original owner which could be confusing or alarming. Obviously this can be misleading and dishonour spirit. However, if the item which is offered to the medium is a family inheritance, such as grandma's ring or grandad's watch, then all the information should be acceptable or can be clarified by another member of the family.

I have tried psychometry but do not feel happy using it. One of the few times I have used it was when asked to assist the Police with a murder enquiry. Then, I asked for an item of property which had belonged to the victim so that I should have some form of contact, and they brought along his walking stick for me. Through this I was able to relate information which I had no other way of knowing and which was later confirmed by the Police as correct. Other times when I have used psychometry have been during group sittings where there has been a situation where one sitter or another has dominated the evening due to having strong spirit links, and by using psychometry it has been possible to help communication between spirit and sitters with weaker links.

Another very popular way of working with spirit is by using the cards. Some mediums use an ordinary pack of cards and read them according to their own interpretation. The most commonly used cards for this purpose, however, are the Tarot cards which many people, even those who are not spiritually aware, frequently use, so caution needs to be observed in consulting someone who truly understands them. They are a very old means of divination indeed with vast spiritual knowledge tucked away within them, but like everything else, used improperly, can alarm people. It is not the accuracy of the cards that is questionable, but the understanding and wisdom of the reader that brings comfort or alarm to the sitter.

There are many very good, genuine people who use the Tarot cards and read them correctly, linking with spirit as well and providing acceptable information. I do find that the Tarot cards can provide good guidance – perhaps in helping decision-making – but they cannot tell you what to do. Like every other form of spirit work, it provides guidance for you, but at the end of the day you must make the final decision. I do possess a pack of Tarot cards (for my own use only) which I rarely use, but occasionally when I am unsure about something I get them out to see if there is any guidance available through them.

Certain mediums do what are called postal readings. My own experiences of these have proved very vague, most of the messages being applicable to several situations. For this form of spiritual communication, you never meet the medium; you are requested to forward a letter or photograph for them to concentrate on, and some ask you for specific questions you need answering. I have sent off for several postal readings but none made any real sense to me as they were too vague for my liking. Although such work is referred to as "psychic work", many use these methods with guidance from spirit, so should not be dismissed.

Another form of psychic work is done by producing what is called an auragraph, from people's auras. These readings explain a great deal and can help since they are very enlightening.

True mediums, to me, are those who work completely with spirit, but also work in different ways.

Let us look first at "mental mediumship". Those mediums who work clairvoyantly *see* spirit and can translate what they see into messages to which the sitter can relate and which he can understand. Clairaudient mediums *hear* spirit and listen to the voices of their guides or the voice of the communicator talking to the sitter. This is the way I work, although I am lucky enough to be able to see as well. Clairsentient mediums *sense* the presence of spirit and what they wish to communicate to a sitter. Clairsentience is something I experience when relating to people's illnesses and methods of passing, and once the sensation I have been given from spirit is relayed to the sitter and accepted as correct, then it is taken away, but if not accepted, then the sensation remains until I have the correct interpretation and it has been accepted.

Some mediums are very lucky and can produce pictures of our loved ones and family in spirit – these mediums are known as "psychic artists" and many work in conjunction with another medium who relays messages whilst the artist is forming the picture. A few well-known psychic artists work on their own and can give off information relating to the person being drawn and thus find the recipient of the picture. To me, this is a very special way of communicating and is to be admired. Physical mediumship, however, is a form of spirit communication with which I am less familiar, but to many this is a more positive means.

Direct voice is communication which occurs when the medium allows the spirit communicator to talk through them directly, whether it is their guide or the spirit person connected to the sitter.

I have experienced allowing my friend, Running Foot, to come through and talk in his own voice. Once again, this was in the early days of my spiritual development and on four different occasions, Running Foot made me aware of his wishes and he always chose late at night when everywhere was quiet. I would set up the recorder and after a few minutes his voice would emerge. I would not be aware of what was said until I replayed the tape. The messages explained his life and work from spirit, but since then there has been no need according to Running Foot to do any further tapes, since he no longer has to convince me that it is his voice I now relate to in my work. Once again we see that everything at that time was done for a definite reason; to strengthen my gift and my connectedness to spirit.

Another form of physical mediumship is materialisation. The medium is usually secured in a chair and the bonds checked before the seance begins, after which spirit manifests as a solid form in the room. This is something I have yet to witness or experience and know only of what I have been told by other mediums who have experienced this; the Noah's Ark Society being instrumental in enlightening people regarding this type of work which is often done in small, private development circles where very spiritually-committed people sit together – sometimes for many years – and work towards developing one of their members to become a physical medium.

These circles are used not only for physical, but also for mental mediumship. In an open circle anyone can come to join with the regular sitters, but there are also closed circles which are kept exclusively for the regulars. Questions being asked by circle members are answered by a medium's guide with teaching from spirit, helping each member to understand more about spirit and spirit work.

As you will see, there are many different ways in which spirit can communicate with us on this earth plane of ours, using those who are able to receive spirit communication and pass on messages not only about spirit work, but letting us know that our loved ones, families and friends are safe and happy in spirit and that they wish to be able to reassure us about the peace and harmony they are now experiencing. Naturally, the stronger the medium's link, the better the spirit communication. Many think that once they are aware, they have the spirit gift and can just give out messages. How wrong they are! A lot of work and dedication has to be given to understanding how to work in harmony with the guides and helpers before treading on the pathway of being a medium.

All the different ways of communication we have talked about can be seen by either visiting a recommended medium for a private sitting, by visiting a spiritualist church or by going to see a medium working in a theatre (but this last way is not always satisfying as the medium does not have the time to go into detail, but will stimulate your interest into taking it a stage further). You can join a development circle either through a spiritualist church locally, or with a reputable medium in a home circle, or perhaps visit a weekend seminar organised by spiritual teachers. All these spiritual links are there for us to have the chance to see if we wish to develop in this way. It is our choice. We have the freedom to go along to see what it is all about and then make any decisions as to whether we wish to learn more, become involved in the spiritualist movement or perhaps to say, "No. It's not really for me," and put it down to an experience from which we may have learned a little more.

Chapter Ten

MORE DETAIL, PLEASE

People often query why communicators do not give more precise detail about such things as their full name, address or telephone number while they were on earth and ask why they do not provide more detail about the spirit world itself. Sometimes they do, but all mediums work in different ways and spirit communicates in the best way they can through any particular medium.

I have asked Running Foot about this and also raised the question with my spirit family and helpers. Running Foot assures me that there are many different ways which spirit uses to pass proof of their life in the spirit world to people on the earth plane.

Each medium works according to their strength and to the direction of their spirit pathway. Running Foot and I work our chosen pathway for spirit; that is, we are working to join the spiritual plane with the earth plane, and to relate to those on the earth plane with messages from their loved ones, their family and friends now in the spirit world.

By doing this, we work on a very personal and often intimate link with people. Firstly, I should like to show you how I communicate with my spirit people and the way we have learned to work together to get the best results.

When I first start a sitting I ask my spirit voice for a link with the sitter. Most times they will give me a month – perhaps their birthday, an anniversary or frequently that which relates to their passing – and once this has been passed on and accepted by the sitter, information usually follows describing how they left us either through illness, accident or other forms of passing which they do not wish to talk about until they know the sitter is relaxed enough to accept. Once this has been achieved and they know that the sitter recognizes the communicator is the person they wished to hear from, more information will be forthcoming. This often consists of the names of family and friends, not just those in spirit but also those still here on the earth plane, each name fitted into place with a little message – perhaps the character of the person, the work they are now doing or hoping to do, whether they have moved house and what kind of house they have now, and especially any little bits of gossip about that person. Sometimes the information relates to romances, divorces or problems around the sitter. Often it is to do with the area to which someone has moved, with details of outstanding features nearby such as a pub, railway, or shop, just to let people know that their loved ones in spirit have visited them.

I find the way I work provides positive identification and is special and familiar. It would definitely be too formal to say simply, "Mr. and Mrs. Jones are here from spirit and want to let you know that they are all right – end of message," when that particular couple were your mum and dad and would certainly not wish to introduce themselves to you in that way.

When we are working with spirit in this manner, I am only a channel for spirit; the messenger who is hopefully relaying the messages, the little pieces of personal information, and trying to link them together properly so that it makes sense to you as the family. There is no set way of working spiritually. Each spirit communicator is an individual. They all wish to come and relate in their own way and style. The medium is the one who sometimes tries to alter the sitting according to the way in which he or she thinks the message should be presented, but if it is not given in the spirit communicator's own phrases and language, it is frequently not accepted by the sitter. People know what phrases were natural to their family and friends, what mannerisms they would have used, how they would react to things and the attitudes they would express when giving help or guidance, and if it doesn't ring true, they are not convinced.

When a person leaves for the spirit world they do not change into a different being; they are still the same, retaining the character they had on the earth plane. Perhaps when they come to advise us they may sound a little more logical, but even so, I find my spirit communicators will want me to explain that if they had still been on the earth plane they would not have seen it that way because they would have been emotionally affected, but now they can see both sides and give advice from spirit. They can show us different sides of situations, not telling us what to do, but perhaps enabling us to view things in a new way, taking into account what we had not considered. However, they only offer help and advice. The decision has always to come from us according to what we feel is the correct thing to do.

As you can see, working with spirit is not just about receiving messages, opening your mouth and giving it out; it's not that simple. You have to work with your spirit communicator. These special people have come to link up with their loved ones and their messages are important. When you are linking with a spirit voice, if you are unsure of what it is they have asked you to say, or feel that it does not sound quite right, you have to ask them to repeat the message or give it in a way you can understand, before passing it on to the sitter. By working in this way you build up a closer and more positive link with your spirit voice and the sitter, as they know you will take your time to give off their messages accurately.

I do my best to make sure that all messages relate to the sitter and are understood, giving off communicators' words sensitively with warmth and understanding, whether it be to pass on love, help or a 'ticking-off', in a way that does not upset their loved one, because I will have waited for the right information before talking to them. Nowadays I find more and more that I have a special link with the younger generation who are in the spirit world, because they know that I am not afraid to interpret them just as they are, with their colourful characters, habits and language. This, to them, is very important – not making them into 'little angels' which they were not when here on the earth plane. They know I will bring through their laughter and allow them to express themselves on such things as teasing their brother or sister, winding up their parents, or whatever. That is who they are and they can still portray their humour from spirit so that you know it is your particular special young person who has not changed; it remains the person we love and miss so much.

Each of these people in spirit has freedom of choice. They will not relate through a medium they feel is an incorrect channel for them to use, but will wait until the right one is available, sometimes manoeuvring their loved ones in the direction of their chosen medium or passing on a message through someone else who has sat with that medium and is able to tell you about it second-hand.

I hope this encourages those who have not yet found a medium through whom their loved ones can communicate with them to continue to search until they do and not give up.

I often ask Running Foot and my spirit family if it is possible to work on a higher level and to be able to relate more detailed information from spirit, but so far we are still working in the same way, as that is the best channel for my personal gift. Perhaps one day spirit and my many communicators will surprise me and give me a telephone number to pass on to their family, or their full names or postal address – you never know!

Having tried to analyse my work, I do find that when I am given a surname in a sitting, it usually relates either to the person's boss or work-friend, or perhaps a neighbour who would be accepted on that basis and not on first-name terms. Occasionally, it is when someone has married into the family and a new name is important. Such things as pubs, holidays and other countries do crop up, but only as memories or perhaps future connections still to materialize. Many times during a sitting, I will ask the spirit communicator to give me more detailed information. Sometimes I am lucky, but mostly the spirit communicator will want to relate in their own way and give off information in their own time, making both the sitter and me wait, because that is how they would have acted when here on the earth plane, but we get there in the end. The loved one, family or friends have the recording on tape and can take it home to listen to and question anything they were unsure about or contradicted at the time. It is not easy to sit and respond speedily to lots of messages, but by taping it, the information is there to think about in a more leisurely way.

Chapter Eleven

HOW LONG DOES IT TAKE?

Questions are important and I always try to make time to answer any which sitters want to ask following a sitting with me. Although sometimes people think I shall find their questions silly, they are certainly not and I don't like anyone to leave feeling bewildered or confused about the way a medium communicates with spirit.

A question which is often asked is, "When people leave us for the spirit world, how long is it before they can communicate with us here on earth?" I only know what I have been told by spirit, and I always stress the fact that my answer is *my* interpretation of what I have been told, and there is no time limit for this. Whether a person in spirit has only just left our earth plane, or has been in spirit for many, many years, what is important is whether we can accept the information which is passed from the spirit communicator to the sitter. Time means very little in the spirit world; it is only here on our earth plane that we have to worry about time, our life here being so often controlled by hours, days and years.

Many people say that when they have been to see another medium, they have been told that their loved one in spirit was too weak to communicate and is needing to rest, or the sitter is informed that they will have to wait for a stipulated period – maybe a year – before their loved one is strong enough to communicate. This is bunkum, but sadly people take note of such things and often do not try to see another medium until such a period is over, suffering unnecessarily in their grief. A lot of times I consider that it is the medium who is at fault, perhaps not having a strong spirit link or just not bothering to take the extra time and energy to communicate. If a sitter comes to see a medium and has a person in spirit who is close to them, that person will not want to let the sitter down and will wish to communicate as a rule. Sometimes there are reasons for not communicating, as those in the spirit world have choice as we do here. It may be that the spirit communicator feels that the available medium is not the correct channel for them to use to pass on their love and messages and they will hold back until their loved one is pointed in the right direction and a medium with whom they can work becomes available. People should not be fobbed off with the excuse that loved ones have not been in spirit long enough to communicate, but should be told that if they try a different medium, then perhaps they may be able to communicate, rather than being left bewildered, distressed and sometimes desperate. Mediums are here to confirm that loved ones are at peace and also to show that there is no such thing as death and, where needed, give guidance and understanding.

In my short time as a working medium, there have been the odd occasions when I have been unable to interpret a communication from spirit correctly. On such times, I try to explain to the sitter why this was; whether it was my fault, or that I felt the spirit person was unsure of my way of working, or didn't like me. Mostly, however, I am able to confirm that the person is in spirit and is at peace. Sometimes the one in spirit wishes only to say, "Hello" and that is the whole message, but I tell the sitter never to give up as people do communicate in their own time and that maybe a different medium might be more able to help. Many people who come to see me tell me that although they have had messages from distant family or friends, they have never heard from the one they most wish to until they visit me, so no doubt their spirit communicator knew I was the right person to translate their messages in a way which would be acceptable to their family, and other mediums no doubt find the same thing.

We all have our own thoughts and ideas about the spirit world. Many do not wish to have those ideas changed. Some people need others to confirm for them what they believe is correct and hope their family will come through to give them the proof they've been waiting for, bringing details of their passing and how they have settled into their new spiritual homes.

As a medium who has worked with so many people from the spirit world, I feel I have a good idea what spirit is all about, and when I talk about the spirit world and the people who live in it, I feel I can give an accurate account of what it is like. If we were all to believe in the same things and saw everything in the same way, there would be no real need for mediums to give evidence of spirit or to relate to spirit communicators. However, because there are those who doubt life beyond death and also people who never give a thought to such things until they lose a loved one, mediums are needed to give help, understanding and support at such times and to provide answers where these are unavailable from other sources.

People have freedom of choice as to what they can accept and believe. Some disbelieve due to religious background, family pressures, or lack of conviction in the truth of what we say, but if we pass on to them what is available from spirit in terms of reassurance of their loved ones safe passage into the world of spirit and their continuing life there, the seed will be planted in their mind to blossom when needed.

I began this chapter trying to deal with the question of how long our loved ones have to be in the spirit world before we can talk with them, and I should like to say that in my own work I have been able to communicate with a person within hours of their passing to spirit and on many occasions before the ritual of their 'send-off' – the funeral – often giving messages of what was happening, even telling the family about the wreaths being chosen for them, all to reassure them that they will not be alone on the day and that their loved ones continue to give them support and love, and hopefully convincing those left behind that they have only left in body, not in spirit.

Some feel they want to see a medium as soon as their loved one has left for spirit, needing the comfort and reassurance of their safe passage into the spirit world. Others need time to adjust and do not require such communication then, but we will always be here as mediums, to help, guide and show that life continues even after the physical body wears out.

Chapter Twelve

YOUNG JACK

I should like to thank Karen for allowing her very special link with her son to be included in this book. I hope this story will act as confirmation of the previous chapter and reassure you that those who have passed into spirit are not prevented from communicating with us either by the short space of time since they passed or, as in this case, by the age at which they did so.

At whatever age someone passes into spirit, those left behind mostly long for reassurance that their loved one has arrived safely in a pleasant situation in the spirit world. Some need that reassurance straightaway, some need time to adjust to their loss first.

Karen first telephoned me in February 1993 requesting a sitting as soon as possible as she had just lost her son. No other information was given to me except that she would like to come before the burial which was to be on the Tuesday, 23rd February, and so a space was found for the Monday evening before the funeral.

I was a little concerned about how it would go, whether Karen would be able to understand the sitting or whether it would prove too emotional for us all, but felt that if she wanted to come, that was all that really mattered. If Karen could be reassured that her son was now at peace in spirit, then we would have helped in some way. She had asked whether her friend, Diana, could sit in with her as she knew what to expect, having been to see me before, so I agreed, and on arrival they were offered tea and coffee while I explained how I work, reminding them that since Diana was in the room, she too would get messages and should answer and correct me if what I gave related to her rather than Karen, so we would keep the messages clear.

The following details taken from the tape which was recorded during the sitting hopefully show that none of us needs to be afraid of communicating with our loved ones, no matter what the situation. Personal messages to the family have been omitted, but true names, dates and situations remain unaltered.

When it was time to communicate with our spirit voices, the first messages that were given were for Diana rather than Karen, mentioning her son on the earth plane, giving information which Diana confirmed. I felt that this was spirit's way of relaxing Karen, showing her that there is nothing to be afraid of. A message from Karen's grandparents followed, sending their love to her in her great need. I was also asked to inform Karen that Chris, a very good friend of hers a few years previously, was with her, offering his support and looking after her son in the spirit world. Chris, who had passed over due to an accident, reminded her that he had known her when she was married, but before her children were born, and that if he had still been on the earth plane he would have given her a big hug. I asked if this made sense to her, and she agreed. Chris gave a big smile and wanted her to know that everyone in spirit was helping her son.

Now the pathway had been cleared and it was Jack's turn to communicate. He relayed that he was actually found because he just 'went to sleep' and that although he was taken to hospital, it was too late, and this was confirmed by his mother. Jack said that when he was first born he did have trouble with his chest but that cleared up, and Karen confirmed this also. Jack then told me that he wanted to explain to her that although his passing had been thought of as a 'cot death', this was not really so, and could she understand this. When she agreed that she could, he said he wanted her to know that he did not suffer and had just 'gone to sleep'.

Jack then asked me to pass on to his mother something which had happened that day, to prove that he knew about it. He tugged the front of my hair and said she used to do that to him and had done so that day when she had gone to see him. Karen confirmed this, and Jack said that although she had seen him, it hadn't really been him, but he understood her need to do so. He just smiled at her and asked for her to be told that he had returned home with her and had come with her tonight.

"So," I said, "all this love is coming through to you at this moment, as Jack knows how it is for you, still trying to realise what is actually happening, because you are still in a daze; and this is why Jack is showing me wheezing with you. It's your asthma again, and it's played you up lately, hasn't it?" "Yes," said Karen. "Jack just wants to reassure you that it will clear up, but it has created a few problems for you." Jack then mentioned his dad and told me that he was self-employed and that Karen was 'sort of'. I asked if this was true, and Karen agreed, and I then added that although his father was all right, he sometimes found things difficult to explain. Jack knew that all the family found it difficult to understand and this made things hard. He then gave me a problem with my neck and his next words made my neck go rigid; he had had meningitis and although no one at the time was aware of this, it was mentioned later. Karen confirmed this.

The next message I related to Karen mentioned the name Allison, a good friend of hers, and I was shown a detached house which she told me was the family home.

By this time, Jack was much more relaxed and I was able to relate freely to him. He mentioned his sister, who is older than him, and started to talk about a particular cuddly toy which he had with him, and when I asked if Karen could understand this, she agreed. Jack then gave me the name Richard, his uncle, and told me that the name Jonathan he was giving me related to his dad. He also mentioned the name Ben, which Karen confirmed as being relevant.

When he gave me a birth date during February, I made the mistake of thinking it was in the present day, but Jack corrected me, drawing my attention to a lady in spirit and telling me that the date belonged to his grandad, Karen's father, who is in spirit, to which Karen agreed.

From then on, Jack reeled off lots of names and information relating to family connections, including Karen's brother and sister, the name Phil or Phyllis, Nick and Matthew (Jack's cousins), Lesley, Alan, and also gave me the name of Harry as being Karen's dad. All these Karen confirmed. He talked about pub work, which Karen said she had done in the past, and gave me a present day birth date in October. Karen agreed, but said that there was one in spirit too, and Jack said, "That's mine."

I had difficulty in understanding why Jack gave me the name of Ted as I had to say, "It's Edward, not Ted" and "It's a second name, but in spirit." Jack said that I was getting nearer, as Edward is his second name, but Edwards was also a surname in the family, and Karen said that this was true. Jack followed this up with the name "Emm" which meant Emily and that she was his sister and was at school, which his mother confirmed. "Jack just wants to say she's pretty," I said, "and that she goes to school." He then told me that Elizabeth was a family name, and I asked Karen whether it is her second name. "No," she replied, "it's my daughter's." Jack was certainly trying his best to give me positive information.

Jack then mentioned the name of Adam, a young child in spirit, which Karen said she recognised as belonging to a family she knows, even though she had not known Adam. He then gave me the name Carly, which belonged to another child in spirit and said that Karen knew both Carly and her family, which Karen confirmed. He just wanted to let her know that now he knew other young people in spirit.

He then said that I had not given his own proper name and that it was Jack Edward and that Karen had called him "Jack the Lad", which his mum said was quite right. (Although I have mentioned him by name throughout this story to make it easier to read, he did not give me his own name until near the end of the sitting.)

During the sitting Jack gave Karen lots of personal information, including mentioning the possibility of moving house, but since the whole sitting took more than an hour, I have only included part of it. The main purpose of this story is to show that this young man was able to communicate with his mother from spirit, before his funeral, even though he had lived on earth for less than eighteen weeks after his birth. We are wrong to think that one so young can only smile at us and gurgle. They understand a great deal about us and the family and can communicate what they know. Since then Karen has also received a message from Jack at a public demonstration saying that she would have another child – which at the time she did not know, but was true. Karen and Jonathan are expecting another child and Jack is looking forward to this, knowing that he is irreplaceable and will always be the special son who watches over them, for ever part of their life.

A MOTHER'S LOVE

The Spirit world must be a wonderful place,
My beautiful Children are in its embrace.
They passed so suddenly, no time for good-bye,
God knows that I sometimes still need to cry.
I ask Him to keep them safe each night,
I worry so much when they are out of my sight.
My son, baby Julian, I was so proud,
Lorraine, a young lady, I still talk to out loud.
Each day I looked for them, each day I'd search,
Then one day I found them in a Spiritualist Church.
My Children are spirit, God made them free,
It was for a short time, He gave them to me.
My memories are good and still make me smile,
I will see them again, though it seems a long while.
Thanks to the people who help me to cope,
And thanks for God's love, He gave me hope.
My heart has been broken, I feel deep despair,
But one day I'm sure He will answer my prayer.
For Mothers who lost precious Children, like me,
Take heart, they're still with us its just we can't see.
I don't think these words were formed in my head,
They poured from my heart in the tears that I shed.

Written by CAROL, *Lorraine's Mother.*

Chapter Thirteen

MY FRIEND, TONY

When people visit me for the first time, it is very satisfying to have their loved ones, family and friends come through, communicating with them, reassuring them of their love and giving off information about themselves together with memories of their lives on the material plane and perhaps quoting important dates such as special birthdays or anniversaries. It is also good when they are able to reassure us that the things we are planning to do are the correct pathway for us to take and can encourage us to progress with all the plans we made before they left so suddenly for the spirit world.

Sometimes, once a person has visited a medium and received the peace and reassurance of knowing that their loved one is all right and still able to hear their voice when they talk to them, they may never again need more communication. They are able to lead their lives peacefully knowing that their loved one is with them and watching over them.

It is much harder to accept when we lose someone very young. Although we may receive communication from spirit that they have arrived safely and may know that they are being looked after by family members already in the spirit world, we may still need communication from that special person; we still worry about them, and although we cannot see or hear them, want to know what they are doing and thinking and whether they are aware of us. To some people in this situation, a medium is their only form of communication and if they find the right one who can communicate quite freely with their loved one, they will wish to visit on a regular basis.

I now have many people who visit my home on a regular basis like this, but I do insist that at least six months elapse between visits, as by then things have happened which give us something to talk about.

At the beginning of my spiritual awareness I would often question spirit whether it was correct for me to continue giving sittings to people I was starting to know well, as I was the spirit communicator. Most times they began to feel just like family and I thought perhaps I should now wean them off, sending them in a different direction. I did not wish to feel that I was of limited help, having passed on everything about their loved ones; their memories, their family connections, and wondering what more could there possibly be to give. I would not want to abuse my gift and just create messages to keep the sitter happy, and I knew I would be very frustrated trying to enlarge on what I had already passed on about the spirit communicator and their family. I would never want to con anyone or give information which had not come genuinely from spirit.

I am glad to say that my fears have proved unfounded. Not only my own spirit family, but also communicators I now regard as my spirit friends, have confirmed that it is important to continue the links with their family; helping to ease their pain and loss until they can accept going on with their own lives knowing that their loved one is still part of them, watching over and listening to them, knowing that when they talk to their loved ones, their voices are heard in spirit.

One of these very special people in the spirit world is Tony, with whom I have been in contact, due to the regular visits from his family, and now regard as a special friend.

Chapter Fourteen

TONY

It was in November 1991 when Tony's parents, Jill and Fred, were to make their first visit to see me. All the information I had was just their first names, and no mention was made of whom they wished to communicate with from spirit.

Jill and Fred were welcomed with the usual cup of tea or coffee and were asked if they would like the sitting to be recorded (which is the way I prefer to work) as this is not only nice for the family to keep, but where information is given off which at the time they cannot place, it is there for them to check up on later.

After explaining to Jill and Fred how I work, it was time to allow spirit to come to join us. Tony – this very special person – came through at the beginning, very positive, confirming that he was their son and sending all his love to them, reassuring them that he was all right. This followed on with Tony giving proof of his passing, stating that it had been "a sort of accident" and that it had only happened a few weeks before, naming the month October and quickly mentioning his uniform; he had been in the navy. He conveyed that he had been killed while serving abroad and that the family didn't know the full story yet. This was confirmed by Jill and Fred.

At this time, Tony was talking very quickly as he wanted to say such a lot and kept jumping from one subject to another, mentioning his grandfather in spirit with whom he had met up, and a friend, who I believe was called "Phil", thus reassuring Jill and Fred that he was not on his own in spirit.

Tony also wanted to talk about his lovely wife, Lorna, and his little son, Danny, and wanted all his love passed on to them, and although he had only left for spirit just before Danny's first birthday at the end of October, he had not missed out on the special day and was with him from spirit. There was such a lot of positive information now flowing from Tony, mentioning Lorna's Scottish connections, and about his in-laws, not forgetting his older sister, Tracy, and his younger brother, Nicky, and talking a little about their characters.

What was so very strong about Tony was his great personality and the way his character came through, especially when he kept on at me to mention his hair and teeth, which made us smile. Also Tony wanted to talk about his "Keep Fit" and his connection with training as a P.T. Instructor, which Jill and Fred confirmed was correct.

All of this time I was aware of what I would call "Tony's cheeky grin" which it appears he always had. At this stage Tony decided to get a little serious by giving me more proof of his passing by mentioning an airman involved in the incident and followed on by showing me a helicopter. This was accepted by Jill and Fred very emotionally; much more personal messages were passed on to his family and Jill and Fred were able to accept a lot of these from Tony although they were still very much in shock at the loss of their special son. Because of this, some information Tony provided did not ring a bell at the time, but when they replayed the tape, most could be accepted.

Since Jill and Fred's first visit that November, we have linked with Tony on a regular six monthly basis. In between, not only has Tony's wife, Lorna, travelled from Scotland to talk with him but also Tony's sister, Tracy, and his brother, Nicky, have paid me a visit, and each time Tony has surprised us with all the updated information which he has been able to pass on, showing everyone that he is watching everything and knows what events are going to come up – especially looking forward to his sister's wedding, informing everyone that he would be there.

The most recent visit from Jill and Fred was on 6th July, 1993, and once again Tony was in his usual good, informative mood, giving his parents positive news about what he knew had been happening and once more talking about Tracy's wedding in Scotland.

After the sitting Jill said, "I have a present for you," and took an envelope out of her bag. On opening it, there emerged a blue-covered book entitled, *Tony's Story* which Jill had written and had had printed as a special surprise for Fred.

That night I read this special book and it was hard not to cry. It is all about Tony's life from being born to his passing into the spirit world. It shows the love the family have for each other and how special Tony was to them. He will never be forgotten. I was honoured to find that Jill had included me in this very personal book. Knowing that I have been able to give a little assistance which has helped to ease their pain and sadness is an honour in itself and I feel lucky to have been chosen to be the connection between Tony and his very special family, who I hope I can now call friends.

With Jill and Fred's permission, I am enclosing the page from *Tony's Story* and I should also like to thank them for allowing me to talk about their visit to me and my communication with Tony.

Chapter Eight – Our lives continue – but never as before
It's now been thirteen months since our darling Tony left us,
how fast the time has gone, I always keep a diary, have done
for years, and since 14th October, 1991 each week I'd add
another week every Monday; the speed with which the year
slipped by was just incredible. I started saying only two
weeks ago Tony was still here, drawing some comfort from
that fact, before I could turn around it was fifty-two weeks
ago. I do believe that the fact that we're kept so very busy has
helped us, we don't have time to dwell on circumstances as
much as we might have if we were in a nine to five situation. I
run the shop with the help of the two Audreys and Fred works
for an engineering company for this area.

We have made fourteen trips to Scotland this year, we go
each time just for the day on the train, leaving home before
six in the morning, having got the papers and shop sorted out
before we leave. The girls and Danny meet us at the station
in Edinburgh we always go straight to Douglas Bank
Cemetery in Rosyth where our Tony is, his grave is in the
military part, up on top of a hill, its very peaceful there,
Danny calls it Daddy's garden, bless him, and likes to help us
arrange the flowers. Lorna keeps the grave lovely, she's
bought two heart shaped vases which are always filled with
fresh flowers; she and Tracy go up every Sunday as do many
of Tony's fellow P.T.I.s from H.M.S. Cochrane. If only Fred
and I lived nearer we would also like to go up every week
and not just once a month as we do at the present.

I must tell you about Brian and the help and comfort he
has been to our family since we lost our Tony. A few weeks
after Tony died I thought of maybe going to see a medium, I'd
only ever been to one once and that was to see Doris Stokes
as part of a mass audience she held in Walthamstow Town
Hall several years ago. I was quite impressed by the evening
and have always kept an open mind on the subject ever since.
A friend of mine's daughter gave me Brian's number and said
she'd heard he was very good and might bring us some
comfort. Fred and I booked up to see him for the first time in
the November after Tony died, he knew nothing about us
apart from our christian names. Within minutes of our
arrival, after he had taken our coats, given us a welcome cup
of coffee and sat us down in his sitting room, he had made
contact with our Tony and was giving us names, dates and
messages from Tony; things that he couldn't possibly have
known, his description of Tony; and his character was

remarkable, even Fred who was very sceptical about the whole visit was reduced to tears as all these details were revealed to us. He told us so many things that we were both quite amazed, there was no answer for it. Since that first visit we go back regularly every six months, so on various occasions have Lorna, Tracy and Nicky. Our meetings with Brian give us a great deal of comfort and make us feel nearer to our beloved son.

Chapter Fifteen

WHAT'S ON THE OTHER SIDE?

Many people have often asked me, "What's it like in the spirit world? Do they have houses to live in; do they have gardens, as many folk have been told? Have they got hospitals and schools, or what do they do?" But mostly, people want to know if they are happy where they are now living.

Many mediums and people who are very spiritually aware seem to have different opinions as to what life in the spirit world is like. Some state that our loved ones do have houses and gardens and have access to the same kinds of material possessions we have here on the earth plane, and then some tell us that there is no such thing. People get rather confused and bewildered and are often left with a false belief as to what they can expect to find when they eventually leave for the spirit world.

Many times I have talked with Running Foot and the other members of my spirit family, enquiring about life in spirit and what they do there. He describes life in the spirit world as full of love, harmony, peace and understanding and talks of the chances we have to advance spiritually, eventually progressing to a higher insight of life and development, as well as having the opportunity of devoting time and energy to helping others, especially those of us still on the earth plane.

To me, these special people, once they have left for the spirit world, become a bright light, an energy force, and this light contains that person's life on earth; their love for their family and friends, their memories and experiences both happy and sad. They now have added insight into our lives and can hopefully offer guidance to encourage us as we progress with our lives and families here on the material plane.

As it has been said many times before, while we are here on the earth plane, our soul or spirit is encased in a material form called the physical body, which is just a casing for the energy form of spirit; this is necessary so that we can transport ourselves about during this period of life on earth. When we have to leave for the spirit world, no one ever dies, it is just our body – the material casing – which dies. We continue to live and are then able to move around in the spirit world without any material help. This is something that people find hard to relate to and that is why, when we communicate with that person in spirit, they portray themself in their earthly body so that we can recognise and accept them, even if it is only their image as when on earth, because many people cannot accept their survival in the spirit world unless they are told what they looked like and can relate once again to an image. As I try to explain to people when I communicate with their loved ones, family or friends in spirit, I prefer to show that person's personality, as to me that never changes and their special ways and expressions are more definite than a changeable image, depending on how they wish to be remembered. We often hold memories of our loved ones as they were just before they left us, and many times the spirit communicator will wish to be shown as much younger; when they were in the prime of life on earth.

Because we have no physical body, we do not need houses, gardens or television, etc., as we did on the earth plane, but once again our loved ones, when communicating from spirit, will want to recreate these images for us and show that they still remember the house, garden and other material things that were very much part of their life then.

When I am linking with these special people in spirit, I often describe the feeling as becoming an energy force like a battery being charged up, then the buzzing begins and the connection is made. The voices then start coming through and the messages are relayed. We are known as mediums because we allow our bodies to be used by spirit.

When our loved ones, family and friends arrive in the spirit world and have come to terms with their new environment, they will always want to let us know that they are at peace and have met up with those who went before. There are some who, once they have found contentment in the spirit world, wish to remain at peace with themselves and do not want to have any communication with us on the earth plane. This is their freedom of choice, such as they would have had while on the earth plane. Happily, mostly you find that loved ones do wish to have communication with us, not only as previously stated, but sometimes to give us the strength to battle on with our lives and perhaps guide us in a more positive direction. No one in spirit can tell us how to lead our lives. However much we might sometimes wish it, they can only guide us. We have to make that final decision to say "Yes" or "No."

As we are all aware, there are many different forms of spirit work and communication. Once in spirit, someone may wish also to venture into more positive work from spirit, as with the wonderful gift of healing which is a very important part of spirit's work. It can bring help and relief to those who are suffering, especially when all other channels of medicine have failed. Very often, you find that a spirit person who is working in healing with a medium on the earth plane, worked in that field in their life here as either a nurse, doctor or perhaps a scientist and wishes to continue that work from spirit, passing on to us their knowledge and guidance in whatever way possible for us to benefit from and put to proper use.

I greatly admire those who are devoted to spiritual healing. Although I have myself done quite a bit of healing with the wonderful help of Kuros, my spirit healer, I now find that it is only a secondary part of my work. I will never turn away anyone if asked, but feel that although it is very nice to be able to say I can do most things for spirit, if I am trying to do too many things at once then I am not allowing myself to be strong in the work spirit wish me to do. This is why in the early stages, I realised that the work in which I wished to excel was as a medium, reassuring people that their loved ones are safe in the spirit world and at peace with themselves. By placing all my energies in this one direction, I hopefully will progress spiritually. I know that we shall never stop learning, and I intend to search further, become stronger, more positive, and understand more about the spirit world, using my gift to help others. So you see, as to everything that is on the other side, we may never fully know until our time comes and we make that journey to see for ourselves.

It is an honour to be trusted with any form of spirit work, but sadly there are those who do not use even this wonderful ability for the correct reasons. They are in the minority and do not serve the spirit world or this; wrongly using the gift to increase their power or wealth by frightening people. Some are given the gift and loose it, some never had it in the first place but have cleverly learned to manipulate words, working on people's vulnerability and obvious responses. Thank goodness, nowadays people are increasingly knowledgeable about spirit and spirit's work, so fraudulent workers do not last long, and the wheat is separated from the chaff. Unfortunately, however, the media always focuses on this side of the work and those who are doing good, true work for spirit are overlooked and very rarely mentioned. That is why I still feel that those mediums who take their gift to the larger venues such as theatres and seminars are doing an important part of spirit work, which gives the public the opportunity to decide whether they believe these things or not, going in the direction they feel is correct for them.

So, my friends, hopefully you will see that there is a great deal going on in the spirit world. We have the benefit of receiving help and guidance and it is up to us as individuals to spread the word of spirit and try our best to help those who are in need.

Chapter Sixteen

TALK TO ME

"Yes. When each and every one of you talks to spirit, we are here listening to your voices, your thoughts and your many concerns."

How often during the day and especially during those lonely nights do we find ourselves sending out thoughts – feeling that we want to talk with our loved ones who have left suddenly and taken that special journey into the spirit world to be united with those who went before. Not only do we want to talk to them of the love we still so dearly feel for them, but we want them to know how much they are missed in so many ways. We want to discuss with them the everyday problems that are causing us concern which we would have sorted out together. We want to talk of the difficult decisions facing us and the dilemmas we struggle with alone, and at such times we long for the special help and guidance which only they could give.

We find ourselves wanting to share with them the happy events and situations occurring in and around the family since their arrival in the spirit world. We want to tell them about the new marriages which have taken place and ask them whether they were present on special occasions with the family. We long to tell them about the new babies born into the world and those expected shortly, and not least, to remember together the special memories of precious moments we shared, the laughter and the tears which, each in its own way, brought us closer together.

We wonder as we talk to our loved ones in spirit whether our words and thoughts *are* being heard, hoping earnestly that one day we shall hear them answer us, bringing us the replies to our many questions, the help and guidance we need and the messages of their love. There are so many things we regret not having said while we were together, not having foreseen that God would call "Time" so unexpectedly to take our beloved family and friends to the world of spirit. We are not only left feeling lost, alone and empty but also frustrated because we no longer know what pathway to follow. That is when our search begins, when we so desperately want our loved ones to hear our voice and for us to hear theirs as they try to reach us with thoughts.

Many people, I am sure, wish they could be lucky enough to have the gift of mediumship to establish the wonderful link with their family and friends in spirit. At times life seems very unfair and we experience a lot of frustration and sadness in missing them. That is when we most need to be put in touch with someone who has the mediumistic gift to enable messages to be passed between them and us, conveying love and guidance as needed.

I find it hard as a medium to try to communicate with my own family and friends in spirit, but although I am lucky in many ways, I would question information I received about them, since I know so much about them. As I lived with my grandparents and looked after them, I might think I was imagining what I wanted to hear about them. I know they are sometimes with me and help me, often visiting me when I am asleep. I take notice of the vivid dreams I remember and put them to good advantage in their guidance for my life.

On several occasions I have visited other mediums in the hope of getting messages from my own loved ones in spirit, but so far, in all honesty, I have received little such acceptable evidence. Maybe they feel I do not need confirmation of their existence because of my own work, but it would be nice to have the contact. Perhaps I too must have patience until I meet with a particular medium who can link up with them.

Often when I give a sitting, I am working with people I have not met before, and when their family and friends come through to say "Hello" and to ask me to pass information to the sitters which is both understood and accepted, then I know I am not 'creating' the person in spirit. Only they could originate such messages and always want people to know they are now at peace, having settled into the spirit world and wanting to reassure us that they hear us when we talk to them and know that we hope to hear their own voices again some day for ourselves.

As on earth, people in spirit have freedom of choice. We cannot go to a medium and demand contact with a particular person. They talk to us in their own time, but usually when you have made a special effort to reach out to them, they will want to make the contact. Many people think we are 'disturbing' them by linking up with them in spirit, but this is not so. They come freely to talk with us. *Your* loved ones will always want to let you know they are safe, take away your fears of having lost them and reassure you that they *are* listening to you.

The truth is that there is no such thing as death. We are greater than our body and it is only the material body which dies. We just leave it behind and advance to a higher state of life.

Chapter Seventeen

DREAMS

At times, each one of us during our life here on the earth plane will enjoy the experience of dreaming. Very often when we awake, we know we have been dreaming but cannot remember the content of the dream, and so promptly forget about it. At other times the dream remains so vivid, so real, that we can remember every detail. It is as if we were actually meeting up in our dream with our loved ones, family and friends who are now in the world of spirit and we miss so much. Sometimes we experience a situation in our dream which is very relevant to our present-day life – perhaps something we have to make a decision about – and our dream conveys an answer to that problem.

When we have such a dream, let us try to accept spirit's help and make use of the message if it makes sense to us. Otherwise, we so often reject the dream as something we think we have imagined and take no notice whatsoever until spirit try to communicate with us again in our dream state, and at last we sit up and take note. It is easy to refuse to believe that our loved ones come to visit us while we are sleeping, because we want so much to hear from them we think we are creating a fantasy with our own minds. However, many times a dream will perhaps give us a quick glimpse of the special person we miss so much and we just get a glimpse of their smile, a brief outline of them which we recognise so well, or perhaps if we are lucky we may hear them pass on a short message, not only of their love but sending us happy words of encouragement to let us know they are still around us.

For the many people here on the earth plane who are unable to communicate as mediums do with spirit, it is during the sleep state that people in spirit can reach them. It is when we are asleep and relaxed, with our minds not focused on everyday thoughts and worries, that we are able to receive those special communications from those now in the spirit world. A lot of people say that the point at which they received that special link was just as they were about to go to sleep or just coming out of sleep and not yet fully awake. However, once our minds become alert, then we question, "Was it really them?" and the more we try to find answers, the more inclined we become to let doubts creep in until we convince ourselves that we imagined it all because we wanted to see and hear them, and that it was not really our special person communicating with us at all. I would like to reassure you that very often it *was* your loved one, family member or friend who made that effort to visit you, to reassure you that they are at peace and happy in their new surroundings and will always remain part of our lives.

A short while ago I experienced a special dream. Previously I had not put much emphasis on dreams and really took little notice of them. This time however, I told the dream to John who encouraged me to write it down as I could not get it out of my thoughts. This I did, very roughly, just as it had happened, and now I am pleased that I did as not only has it proved something to me, but I shall take much more notice of dreams in the future and not reject them until I have understood what possible meaning they have for me.

Although I work with spirit, I find it very difficult to use my gift to help myself. At times I am very stubborn and automatically assume that any answer which matches what I want is due to my having influenced it. However, I know that in my sleep state I do not, so I now hope that spirit are getting through to me and giving me the help I need in this way. I hope that putting the dream in the book and relating what happened, may help other people to think about situations where they have not been convinced that spirit were using dreams to communicate with them.

At first my dream was very difficult to accept because the person who visited me that night was not a member of my family, nor even a friend to whom I could relate. This rather special spirit gentleman was a very respected spiritual person who had left us suddenly for the spirit world only a few months before. He was none other than Gordon Higginson who had come to visit me in my home.

I recall that we were in the sitting room which is where all my sittings take place, and I remember Gordon saying that he had come to collect something. At this stage I can remember handing Gordon a silver-backed hand mirror as found on a lady's dressing table. On turning over the mirror, it was marked with small black patches as if, through age, it had lost some of its use. As all of this was happening, we sat and talked for a few minutes and I recall that Gordon asked me what I was doing on the 1st and 2nd of May, to which I replied, "Nothing." This was followed by him asking me where I would be working the coming weekend, and I stated that I would be in Nottingham. By this time we seemed to have left the sitting room and arrived in the hallway. As we stood talking, I can remember thinking, "Why has Gordon got a carrier-bag in his hand with what appears to be towels in it?"

At this stage we both focused our eyes on the ceiling where there was a hole with water flowing slowly from it which gradually became more intense before suddenly stopping. I remember turning to Gordon and remarking, "That's always happening. I really must get it fixed." Then Gordon looked very relaxed but strangely appeared unshaven, which was an image very few people who knew him would ever see, as he was a very immaculate person and always looked very much the gentleman. Gordon's next words were, "I had better go now, as I am not supposed to be happy yet." And then he smiled at me. For some strange reason, I was made aware of a dog that was in the car which Gordon had outside, because I remarked to him that if he wanted, he could give his dog a walk around the farm. In the next piece of information, the conversation had switched to Gordon mentioning his church and where it was, and with that, Gordon had gone.

This dream took place on the Saturday night, and on the Monday, I was working away at one of my favourite churches, Witham Road Spiritualist Church, Sheffield, giving private sittings throughout the day. We had finished during the early evening, and since by the time we got home all the fish and chip shops would be closed, we decided to stop at Retford, get our supper and visit John's family, so it was rather late when we finally reached home, rather tired.

On arriving home, the telephone was flashing, so we thought we had better listen to the messages before retiring. The first message was from my sister informing me that my father had been taken into hospital with a stroke, and as we listened to the remainder of the messages, I could feel drops of water on my head, and there, right above me, was this small hole through which water was dripping steadily to the floor. Looking down, the carpet was quite wet; water had been dripping for quite a while. The hot water tank had sprung several holes and by now the water was coming through much more quickly and another hole began to appear. Everything was therefore quickly dealt with, the water cut off and attempts made to drain the tank. Although I thought we had stopped the flow, the tank was not completely empty and the water was still coming through the ceiling. We managed to contact a local plumber who, I am very grateful to say, came out although it was nearly midnight, and was able to make sure that although we were without water for the next forty-eight hours, the house was safe until he could come to install a new tank.

Straightaway my thoughts went out to the dream which I had experienced two days earlier. As Gordon had had a stroke, so had my father, and on the same day that the water appeared through the ceiling. I cannot help but think that spirit, through Gordon Higginson, had tried to forewarn me and I am sure it helped me not to panic nor get uptight with the situation. I feel also that the event was to make me more aware of future dreams as another positive form of communication from spirit, because being spiritually aware I am inclined not to use my gift to get messages for myself, feeling that perhaps I would influence any message and doubt the answer. I hope that because of this, spirit will pass their messages for me in the sleep state using dreams.

The interpretation regarding the silver hand mirror with the black patches, according to friends who also work spiritually, may be regarding areas of spirit which I have yet to experience and that as I progress spiritually, the meaning will eventually become clear. I hopefully will reach a peak of spirit development and should like to believe that Gordon, in some small way, is helping me, as he will many others, from his new life in the spirit world. The reference made to the 1st of May concerned the date in 1986 when I first became spiritually aware, so I now look forward to further communication from spirit, hoping that more material from this special dream will become clear, and I hope that future contact with Gordon Higginson will also be possible.

Since this episode, one other notable event occurred to me. We had arranged a demonstration in a local theatre, and due to the local paper giving us very little support or publicity in the town preceding it, the ticket sales were very low when we checked and I was expecting very few people to attend. However, that night spirit kept repeating the number "180" to me and so it continued throughout the rest of the week. On the night of the demonstration, exactly 184 tickets were sold, and with those who had complimentary tickets, etc., the seating was three-quarters full and we had a very enjoyable evening. Once again spirit was showing that they can give positive help and reassure me that we are all working together for the same aims; helping others through spiritual awareness.

Chapter Eighteen

BE YOURSELF

It is funny how, once you start putting pen to paper, the stories appear! Recently, I drove to Wales to visit two very special friends, Karen and Sharon, in whose home I was to give some private sittings while I was staying there, for which I was very grateful.

On my journey, I found myself recalling an episode which had been triggered by hearing of the sudden passing of Gordon Higginson. Gordon was one of this century's great workers for spirit. He was a great ambassador for our movement and a liberal spokesman who took spiritualism to wherever it was welcome.

If we are honest with ourselves, at times we often admire other mediums and people who work endlessly for spirit, wishing we could be as good as they are or able to work as they do.

The event I was remembering took place in May 1992. I was going to my first spiritualist rally and it was to take place in the Assembly Rooms in Derby. On arrival, my fellow mediums, John, Diana and Jackie, and I consulted the day's programme to plan what we each wanted to see and decide on the lectures we wanted to hear. Having sorted that out, we strolled around the many different stands and chatted to old friends we normally only meet at different churches served throughout the year. Near lunch-time, I bumped into a lady I had not seen for a few years and we stood talking at the top of the stairs, when a smart, well-dressed gentleman appeared smiling and came over and shook hands, saying, "Nice to see you. I hope you enjoy your day," and walked away. Yes, that was Gordon Higginson who I had never met before, having been in spiritualism myself for such a short period without attending any meetings or workshops where I would meet such people. I was very impressed by this man's naturalness and the calm he radiated; I knew that to attend Gordon's demonstration of mediumship that evening would be an experience in itself.

A lady named Kath Baker was in charge of arranging private sittings, and during the afternoon approached me to ask if I would be willing to help them out as they had more people wanting sittings than the existing mediums could cope with. This was another "first", as I had given hundreds of private sittings, but never in such a situation and atmosphere with so much noise and people passing by continuously. I really wondered how I would be able to concentrate, but once I started, I was oblivious to everything but the sitter and the messages, and the next three hours flew by. I did not manage to attend any of the lectures but I really enjoyed the experience and afterwards, I managed to get a quick cup of tea and a sandwich before the final event of the day, the evening demonstration by Gordon and other members of the S.N.U.

Each medium was allocated a set time to demonstrate, showing their own personality and evidence from spirit. When it was time for Gordon to take the stage, he came on to a standing ovation and then it was down to business. All of a sudden the evening came alive for me; the feeling and atmosphere was magical. Gordon's personality shone through, as did his sense of humour, and most important of all, was the accurate and positive evidence he gave. I was glued to my seat and completely enthralled with every word and gesture; the laughter and reassurance Gordon created was there for all to see. As I sat there, I made up my mind that this was how I wanted to be and hoped that one day I might be just as good.

On the way home all the conversation was about our day, with Gordon's appearance as the main topic. I was already trying to work out in my mind how I could change my own way of working.

The next night, which was a Sunday, I was due to serve Newark Spiritualist Church, and when I arrived I thought, "Right. Tonight I will try to be a Gordon Higginson and work as he does." Well, I couldn't have made a more disastrous mistake in not being myself and trying to be someone else. Although the messages were accepted, everything was as flat as a pancake and I was aware of struggling with each message. My confidence was waning and I was most definitely not enjoying my evening. It was such a relief when it was time to sit down and go home.

I returned home dejected and very disillusioned about my work, and at that moment was sure I would not demonstrate any more. The next day, however, I was more rational and felt better after meditating. The boss, Running Foot, told me why it had gone wrong and I had not been able to give my best. He explained that to work with spirit you must be yourself and that was why I had been given this wonderful gift of mediumship. By experiencing the episode, spirit knew I would learn a little more and will now always be myself, so the bond with spirit can be much stronger.

This experience had shown that by being natural with your gift, spirit will always be there to help and guide you. If you do get a little out of your depth by trying to be too clever, the messages will still be there but the positiveness will be weak and the presentation sadly lacking, even though spirit will never let you down and will still stand by you. I feel therefore, that this very brief, chance meeting with Gordon Higginson has in some way improved my awareness and hopefully enabled me to help other people too, so we can all learn a little more. Having learned my lesson from this episode, when asked for advice on the subject, I always say, "Be yourself. Feel from the heart and try to blend your own personality with your gift of spirit. Enjoy every moment of the wonderful opportunity you have been blessed with." It is so important that when we work with the lovely people in spirit who wish to come to join us and pass on their messages of love, help and guidance, they be allowed to come through as naturally as possible, as we would have known them when on our material plane.

I have been a spiritualist for a very short time – only seven years – and did not develop through a circle and had no previous teaching, knowledge or experience, but was able to link immediately with those in spirit and work for them. Because of this, some people may believe me incapable of advising others and unable to criticise or condemn things which I feel to be questionable in the work some people do for spirit. I feel however, that in my very brief work for spirit, they have given me the knowledge and a great deal of experience with the intensity of private sittings, church services and public demonstrations which I have been asked to do; as much as many people do in a lifetime.

We as individuals, have been given this spiritual gift to enlighten people who are unsure, to help those who are suffering, and to show that there is no such thing as death. People try different ways to develop the gift and there are things to be said for and against these ways.

Many who wish to learn more about spirit and spiritual truths find books or involvement in a good development circle necessary and important in order to get their questions answered and gain reassurance and direction on their pathway, so that their spirit gift will blossom. I know and understand that development circles are necessary to many people, especially those hoping to further their gift and understand more about spirit. However, I have noted that in some situations, a few mediums who have developed through these circles, seem afraid to be themselves on the platform and tend to keep within the framework they have been taught by the medium in charge. By this, I mean that they give off messages in the same way and with the same phrasing they have been taught and are afraid to put the message in their own words and interpret it themselves. Each medium has the ability to be an individual and express their work naturally, as spirit wishes it to be. It is wrong to dictate to pupils that they must work in a certain way, which only produces an extension of the original medium.

I regard myself as a natural medium. Having been made aware of spirit, I was able to accept my gift and use it straightaway. I never doubted what had been given to me, and was from the very beginning eager and willing to learn more, not from books or other people, but from getting on with it and gaining experience through my spirit work. If I was unhappy about any aspects of the work, or felt I should question things which didn't seem quite right, I would listen to other people's views and advice and then meditate with my spirit family. I would sit and ask them for answers to these doubts and ask for guidance. They never let me down. Sometimes they would make me experience things first and then enlighten me afterwards as they knew that experience gives the extra understanding necessary to help certain people. We can all stand up and try to give advice, but when you have been through life with all its ups and downs, often having found yourself in similar situations, and know the feelings of despair or loneliness, it helps greatly in relating to those seeking such guidance. Because of this, I do sometimes find difficulty in understanding certain things about what are considered proper ways of working for spirit, because things have been written about or "always done that way". None of us can say that there is just one way to work spiritually. We all have to be treated as individuals and encouraged to explore our own natural way of expressing ourselves. Spirit will always guide us as long as we are freely wanting to work with them, but we must be true to ourselves; it only gives spirit a bad name if we try to act as someone we are not capable of being.

It is never easy to stand in front of people anxiously waiting for you to give them evidence of spirit. I am sure we all know that a few people will always want to see you make a fool of yourself, or look for things to criticise; this is part and parcel of the work we take on. Although you know what is right, some can never be convinced. For mediums who have built up a reputation for their work, this situation becomes much harder, for even within the spiritualist movement envy creeps in and people cause trouble. Sadly, this seems to be happening lately with quite a number of churches and they are in danger of becoming no better than other religions who are fighting amongst themselves for power.

Many very good mediums work quite happily in their own environment, just serving local churches and doing a marvellous job, keeping the extent of their spiritual work within limits due to other commitments. Other mediums are stimulated to expand their gift, wanting to progress and take it into wider horizons such as theatres, halls and maybe television. Sadly, there are still some in the spiritualist movement who condemn them, criticising them for making money out of their gift. What they do not seem to understand is, that if it was not for these people, many would never be aware of spirit. From my own experience, a lot of those who attend a theatre demonstration would never venture into a spiritualist church or visit a medium, but from the experiences of that night, will become less afraid of spirit. They will often want to know more and can be directed to their local church or meeting place. There will, no doubt,

86

always be people whose goal is to cash in on such events, giving spirit a bad name, but people nowadays are not so easily led and pick and choose. The public always spreads about the name of a good medium who is worth going to see; good always overcomes evil.

Not every medium is able to be so positive as to relate names, months and perhaps telephone numbers at a demonstration, but are still able to give evidence to bring comfort and guidance to those in need. It does, however, concern me when I have visited churches and demonstrations, to see working mediums giving off such vague spirit messages that almost the whole congregation would be able to find something relevant. The message is phrased in such a way that it can be fitted to more than one answer, so if the first one is not accepted, it is twisted to make it fit. People are not fools and see this.

Many attending a service or demonstration are very vulnerable, desperately wanting either help or a message; they can be easily led as they want to accept things, which is not what spirit is for. There are certain mediums who once on the platform, are never wrong. If they come to you with a message and you cannot accept it, they will argue and try to badger you into accepting it. I have seen mediums stay with one person for over twenty minutes arguing about the message and insisting that their message from spirit cannot be in question. Once again, this is not true spirit working. Mediums who do not give the recipient time to answer when delivering a message may in the end have passed on a message, but none can judge whether they were right or wrong. This is not true spirit work, as all messages should be accounted for. If the medium is getting a message from a spirit communicator, it should be for someone specific in the room and be accepted by them. Whether the medium is clairaudient, clairvoyant or clairsentient, when linking correctly with spirit, they should be able to know who the message is for and interpret it as well as possible. Spirit would not waste time and energy linking with us if there was no one to accept their message. On occasion, a message is not meant for the person receiving it, but that is only when the spirit communicator knows that the receiver will be able to pass it on to their loved one who, for some reason, is unable to be present. Spirit will always use any possible channel if they know that it will help those in need, or spread the message of spirit to all parts of the world.

Whatever stage we may have reached spiritually as a medium, healer or worker for spirit, we should never sit on our laurels and think, "OK. We have the gift and that's that." We should all want to improve our link with spirit, see what more there is to learn and how we can do better. We cannot demand that spirit works with us, but working with spirit is a lovely freedom of choice. It is the joining of the two worlds in love, harmony, peace and understanding. I am pleased that I had the privilege of meeting Gordon Higginson and of seeing him demonstrate his wonderful gift of mediumship. Sadly, I never had the chance to see another great ambassador for spirit, Doris Stokes, who comes from the same town where I was registered, Grantham. Unfortunately, Doris left for the spirit world one year after I became spiritually aware.

These people are legends of spiritualism and can never be replaced. It is inevitable that people are often ready to put other mediums on their thrones and state that so-and-so will be the next Doris or Gordon; no one can ever take their place. They have made their mark for spiritualism in this century and will always be remembered for their gift and their individual personalities. Regrettably, there are those who are eager to raise their voices only to snipe at them now they are no longer here to answer those who accuse them. The majority of spiritual people, however, knew their work and know that they would not have been at the forefront of spiritualism had their gift not been pure spirit.

Chapter Nineteen

THOSE WHO LEAVE US BY THEIR OWN HANDS

We all find it very difficult to accept whatever way our loved ones leave us to make that special journey into the spirit world. Lately, I have become more and more concerned with people's attitudes towards those who take their own lives. It is difficult enough for any of us to come to terms with, without being complicated by negative views from those in authority.

I find it very annoying when those left behind are caused even further anguish by people – even those in our own movement – who pontificate about it according to their own particular religious beliefs, whatever they may be. Many of us have very conflicting views and loved ones are often left confused, frightened and sometimes bitter towards those they have loved who have committed suicide.

People who have, for whatever reason, decided to take their own life and join family and friends already in the spirit world, are not mad, nor should they be treated like criminals because of their action. At that time of their life, it appeared to be the correct decision to make. They felt it was perhaps their only answer, not wishing to remain on our material plane. Most of them, when they communicate with us, explain their reasons, even though we may not be able to accept them.

I have tried to reunite many families who have lost someone special in such a way, and would like to share what I have learned from spirit about this matter, having talked to many who made that decision and have communicated from spirit about it. Hopefully, this will answer many questions and remove fears and anxieties for those who have serious doubts about people who have left us in this way.

Usually, following a sitting with those who have lost someone through suicide, I try to talk to them and answer any doubts and questions still in their minds. Many find great relief as they have been told quite frightening things and have been misinformed about what happens to such people once they have left for the spirit world.

Families have told me that they have been told (often by people involved in our movement, supposedly spiritually aware, and usually working mediums) that their loved one will have been sent to a lower level in spirit for having taken their own life. On asking my spirit friends, I am told that there is no such place, and the information I have been given from spirit is that following a person's suicide, they were met with love and understanding from their family and friends already there. They tell me they were helped to come to terms with their transition from our earth plane to their second home in the spirit world. Sometimes, younger ones who took their life, say that not only were they met with love, but they also got a "ticking off" from a grandparent, as they would have done had they still been on the earth plane. So we see that even there, life is not so different.

I also find it very disturbing when people are informed that loved ones have not made the transition from the material plane to the spirit plane and are wandering about as a sad, lost spirit; often the word "haunting" is referred to, and to me, this is not only dreadful but incorrect. I can honestly say that every person I have spoken to who has previously committed suicide (and they are numerous) has confirmed that they arrived safely and were met with love and understanding. No one is ever rejected, whoever they may be.

In my experience with people who have taken their own lives, almost all have told me that they made the choice believing it was right for them, desperately wanting peace of mind which seemed impossible to achieve here on earth. Many people will passionately argue with me on this, but I believe that a person leaves because it is their time to, and progress on to their next stage in spirit. It is just that we cannot accept it because we are brought up to believe that illness, disaster or accident are the only ways we should leave this life for spirit.

If someone attempts to take their own life, and it is not their time to leave us to join spirit, they are found and saved, as they still have more to experience, learn, and achieve before spirit calls them. These people are always crying out for help and usually their method of attempted suicide is an overdose of pills and drink or cutting their wrists incompetently which they know is not instantaneous and, deep down, they know they will be found. It is their cry for help and understanding.

However, those that are sure it is their time to leave for spirit will carefully plan their passing, usually very secretly, having thought of every possibility to make sure no one is around, and the way they leave us is quick and positive and absolutely effective with no chance of escape. Such people have planned their passing for weeks in advance and take what they feel, at that time, is the correct decision to end their life on this, our earth plane.

Since this is the way I see suicide, I find it very sad that when we look to religious authorities of various sorts for help and comfort on our loved ones' passing, so many of them make matters much worse by making statements to the effect that they have committed a sin and cannot go to heaven (nonsense) and make us feel guilty for not having prevented it, so making our suffering greater, rather than giving support and comfort. Those of us left behind believe we have let them down, and feeling guilty and frustrated, attempt to blame ourselves. We begin to feel, very often, that maybe if we had given that person a little more of our time, taken more notice of them and their problems, been more aware of their depression, their failure to resolve a quarrel or some such problem, we might have prevented them making that decision. These are just a few of the torments we suffer, and when I link with these special spirit people, they always want to reassure us about their reasons for their choice and explain that whatever part we had in that decision, it was only part of the picture.

I find these people do not blame anyone else, but sometimes feel annoyed for the hurt and sadness they have left behind due to their own inability to sort out their lives and come to terms with themselves. In my ongoing work with spirit, I still believe that the person who left us for whatever reason, be it emotional, financial, or through fear of illness, arrives in spirit at their right time.

Many see suicide as running away from life and responsibility, being left by a loved one to face up to problems alone and to bring up families on their own, struggling to live as normal a life as possible. In such situations, many people find it hard to talk to others about what has happened; feeling it is a family stigma, many suffer inwardly and shut themselves off from others and feel bitter towards their loved one for creating the situation.

The person who has moved into spirit often feels sad at being rejected and finds it difficult not to be able to communicate with us on earth to explain, even though they understand the feelings of those left behind. A frequent example of such a situation is with a young person in spirit whose father is unable to accept the fact that his son committed suicide, being afraid to show emotion or forgiveness; it is as if, being a man, they feel they have an image to maintain. Thank goodness it is not always like this. When fathers or other members of a family react like that, friction is often caused within the group and splits people apart rather than bringing them together. Fortunately, most families unite in such situations and support each other.

Having shared with you my involvement with spirit in trying to help others understand this most difficult part of life, I should also like to share with you the fact that I have been "on the other side of the fence" twice in my life when I was younger. I felt the need to take my own life and attempted suicide. Both times I was saved and my friends helped greatly. Sadly, I cannot say the same for those in authority who could have helped but made me feel like a criminal. Until you have experienced these things in life, you cannot judge, so I feel I understand these special people more than most. They know I will interpret their messages with understanding and never stand in judgement.

Chapter Twenty

THE POLICE

When I give people sittings, I ask them if they would like it recorded, or if they would like to take notes. Following a recent incident, I am very glad I do.

Some time ago, I had just arrived home from shopping. My first sitting of the day was due to start at 12.30 p.m. and I thought, "Good. I can relax and read the paper before then." I had just made a cup of tea and settled down to read the paper when there was a knock on the door. John Brett, who was with me at the time, answered the door to a gentleman who asked if I was in and whether he could have a word with me. John asked who he was and what he wanted but received no reply. The man came into the room and said to me, "I'm a detective," and informed me which station he came from and asked whether I could spare him a few minutes. We went into the sitting room where he was given a cup of coffee. The detective then said, "It may seem a strange request, but we would appreciate your help." So, of course, I said "Yes".

Well, the story was about a sitting I gave to a lady over six years ago and it concerned her missing husband. It was one I shall never forget, as it was at the very beginning of my work as a medium and in those days I never charged for sittings. It was the first time I have ever told someone that their loved one was no longer with us. As she had brought his wallet for me to have contact with, I worked with it to help my link with spirit. I always say to people before I start the sitting that I can never tell that anyone is going to die, but once they have passed into spirit I can relate to them. This time, it was absolutely positive that her husband was in spirit. He gave me details of his car, that it was to do with the docks, and I experienced his death and the murky water, even knew the area to look in. I was told that this agreed with the thoughts the Police had on the matter, as her husband had not taken anything with him, no money or clothes, just gone out in the car. This sitting took place just a few weeks after it had happened, with a lady (who was either her sister or her friend) writing everything down. It was an emotional sitting, not only for the ladies but also for me, as it was the first time I had told anyone that their loved one had passed into the spirit world. What little else I remembered of the sitting regarded his family and their problems.

The other reason I had not forgotten this sitting after a gap of six years was that a journalist was involved. I had been approached by the local paper to be given an interview by the editor, Richard Reed, who had heard of my work and wanted to do a feature on me. Richard was due after this sitting but arrived a little early, so I made him a cup of coffee and he waited in the next room. I returned to conclude the sitting. The ladies, who were very tearful, went up to the bathroom and finally left. Richard, being a typical journalist, had not missed much and asked whether I could tell him anything about the sitting, which I refused to do, except to say I had to tell the woman her husband was in spirit, but that was all. In his opening article, the first part of the story contained Richard's impression of that moment, but no more was said about the husband's disappearance and I gave the matter no more thought.

It appeared that the detective wanted to see me because this lady had remarried and moved away from the area. While sorting out old papers, she came across the notes of the sitting made six years before. At the time of her husband's disappearance, she had not told the Police she had visited me and decided, after reading through the notes, that she would send them on to the Police. Her husband's body still had not been found, and I suppose the matter was still on police files.

Now the story gets more intriguing. It appears that, about nine months after the disappearance, the Police received an anonymous letter suggesting they should look closer into the family, especially at his son and two friends, who were arrested but no charges made.

At this stage the detective asked me whether I had written the letter as it had a Grantham postmark (which is our area) and saying that it was not a crime to send an anonymous letter. Of course, I had no hesitation in saying, "Definitely, no." I would have had no reason to do such a thing, and in any case after that period of time details of the sitting were vague and nothing to do with me.

The detective then asked if I could show him some of my handwriting which I gladly did and on looking at it and comparing it with a letter he had in his folder, said, "It's no way the same." Then he proceeded to ask me if I would write something down for him. He handed me a sheet of paper and a pen and dictated a sentence which I wrote down and handed to him. His comment was, "Some of it looks similar," and no more was said.

The detective also asked if I could remember much about the sitting, to which I answered honestly, "Very little – only the difficult moment of confirming that her husband was in spirit." Then the detective informed me that in the notes made by the ladies at the sitting, I had told them that two men and another person were involved in something regarding the husband, but stated that no crime had been committed. (This, obviously, was what he was referring to about the son and two other people.) Since the sitting had taken place so long before and the notes had just been found and handed to the Police, it confirmed that the sitting was correct at the time and that spirit knew what would happen about it.

The detective then talked in general about my work; he had been involved with a previous case – a murder – on which I had also worked with the Police. I commented that if the Police asked for my help, I would give it, but would never go to them with information, which surprised him and I don't really think he liked it, but I feel that approaching the Police with information makes you look suspect yourself.

After a short period of very casual chatter the detective thanked me for my help and departed, as my next sitter had arrived. So far, I have heard no more of this incident, but it is early days yet. This situation certainly goes to show that as a medium, we carry quite a lot of responsibility, and what is told to a sitter should be recorded or understood by the person before they leave, so that they do not go away feeling confused, frightened, or afraid of the work of spirit in helping us here on the earth plane.

Gifted Bryan goes beyond the grave
by
Richard Reed

The muffled sound of a woman crying filtered softly through the door.

She was sobbing in a strange, strangulated voice as she fought to hold back the tears.

I waited alone in silence. Here, in the cheery, chintzy kitchen, everything seemed incredibly ordinary – except for that voice.

The only thing to betray events on the other side of the door were a few copies of *Psychic News* scattered on the plain wooden table.

Eventually the crying ceased, and after a short interval I was shown into the sitting room.

Tears too, stood out in the eyes of medium Bryan Gibson. He had obviously been deeply affected by what had just passed.

Prejudice
He told me a little, not wanting to prejudice the woman's

confidence. Her husband had been missing for some weeks, and she wanted to know where he was.

"I had to tell her he was dead," said Bryan. "It came through so strongly."

His conviction was as deep as his sorrow for the woman's suffering, yet she had obviously sought his help to end the terrible uncertainty

Bryan Gibson's uncanny ability to make contact with the spirit world does not just enable his clients to reach the dead.

Being on the "other side", the spirits are able to give a glimpse of things to come – and offer advice from their superior vantage point.

Bryan Gibson's gift is prodigious. His fame has spread so rapidly that since starting out as a medium fifteen months age, he has seen more than one thousand people.

Already he is booked up until January – yet he does not advertise. All the people who come to see him have done so purely on the recommendation of friends or relatives.

Even more unusually he refuses to take money for a sitting.

Wrong reasons

"I have found that a lot of people who charge are doing it for the wrong reasons," he said.

"It's a gift you have – it annoys me when people abuse it. When you only have yourself to look after, money is secondary. You don't need much money to get by."

Bryan – who will only say he is in his forties – lives in a lovely old farmhouse in Kirkby-le-Thorpe.

But although he has spent the past twenty-five years in London, his roots are firmly in Lincolnshire.

Born in Claypole, near Newark, he was registered at Grantham – the same as Britain's most famous and much-loved medium, the late Doris Stokes.

Perhaps that is no coincidence. There is something about Bryan that makes it seem as if he were meant to follow in her footsteps. Nation-wide acclaim cannot be far away.

The gift came to him very suddenly – within a week, in fact.

Spiritually aware

He went to the Spiritualist Church in Sleaford where another well-known local medium, Joyce Gearing, told him he was very spiritually aware, and should develop it.

She told him who his two main spirit guides were –

Running Foot, Sioux Indian Chief who died in 1822, and a Greek-Egyptian boy named Kuros from before the time of Christ.

Bryan sat down one night and tried to make contact with Running Foot. At first, all he saw was a pair of eyes looking at him.

See things

"I said, 'you want me to see things.' And then as pictures came into my mind that night, I said what I was seeing, and if they were correct, I would nod."

On the second night he had to recognise different sounds that came to him. Then, on the third and fourth nights, the pictures and the sound came together.

"It was like looking at a movie and seeing everything fitting into place," said Bryan.

On the fifth night, he heard Running Foot's voice for the first time.

"I never had any awareness before that," he said. "Yet within the space of three weeks I was able to sit down and tell people things about their lives."

His clients are of all ages and from all backgrounds. They don't always find what they expect.

"Sometimes people are scared," he said. "Some people even think I can only work at night!"

Yet Brian uses no crystal ball, no ouija board, no paraphernalia at all. The only unusual things in the room are an amazing collection of pottery cats, and a striking drawing of Running Foot, his guide.

He sits and talks to the spirits of the dead with an air almost of nonchalance – as if they were sitting in the chair next to him, as I was, chatting over a cup of tea.

Togetherness

"My guides are my family, I work with them all the time. It's togetherness. I am not using them for a reason – they only come down because they want to help," he said.

There is nothing frightening about a sitting – except the incredible accuracy with which he recounts details of your life.

Certainly what he told me was enough to convince me that he has a remarkable gift. The most ardent sceptic could not doubt that there is something extraordinary at work here.

"I do not tell people what to do – I tell them what is

possible for them," said Bryan.

"When people come to me, I always explain how it works. It must be very strange for people if they have just come here and I start saying things without explaining what I am doing.

"The truth is very important in this work. If it's not there, I do not give it . . . There's such a lot you can help people with."

Bryan can not only talk with the dead – he can also "tune in" to the living, and tell you of friends you may not have seen in years.

But undoubtedly his most potent gift is his ability, through the spirits of the dead, to predict the future.

He told one young motorcycle racer he would win a T.T., and he duly did.

He told a single woman in her late forties she would be married inside a year – and she was.

Already people are coming to see him from all over the country, and even one or two from abroad.

By using his healing guide, the boy Kuros, he has been able to relieve much physical – and mental – pain.

Sceptical

Since I seemed a little sceptical, he offered to show me. He held his two hands rigidly either side of my own hand – not touching, but at least six inches apart.

He concentrated for a moment, and I felt my hand begin to glow with heat.

"It's like being taken over," said Bryan. "He guides my hands over the person's body – though I never actually touch them."

"People say they can feel the heat – and the pain going away. I've had people with joints that were completely seized up who were able to move them afterwards."

Bryan can also diagnose illness even if people are not aware of it.

He told one woman who had a breast lump not to worry because it would be contained – and it was.

But what of the ethics of what he is doing? Many church leaders would condemn his work.

"Jesus died – and was resurrected. He talked to the dead, and even brought the dead back. I am doing no more than that."

Devil worship

"You will always get devil worship. If you believe there is

evil, you will create evil. You can always create monsters."

Even Bryan does not know why his life has been transformed so dramatically.

"What I have done in this year is so sudden and so instant there must be some reason for it," he said. "But I can't give that reason. I have to wait for it to come to me."

One thing is certain, Bryan Gibson is a name you will be hearing a lot more of in the years to come.

Chapter Twenty-one

LIZ BUTTERFIELD

In my work, I meet many different people from all walks of life, displaying varying talents in differing fields.

What follows is the story of a lady called Liz Butterfield who first visited me for a private sitting in December 1992 returning a couple of months later to bring her son, Chris, for a sitting of his own.

Liz is a freelance commercial artist who specializes in animal portraits and who designs ceramic plates for collectors which are now very popular. Liz will have a go at almost anything though and likes to experiment with her gift. Her work is both remarkable and beautiful and is created with such love that the life within it touches you.

On her visit to me in June 1993, Liz brought some of her work to show me, some of which had just been finished. One particular painting that caught my eye was of a beautiful fairy sitting amongst some crocuses on the edge of a field, her dress made from crocus petals. In one hand she holds an apple, and on the other, there sits an owl, while she gazes at a bright lotus-flower sun.

After her sitting, Liz stayed for a coffee and we began to talk about my work and about my book. She mentioned that she had made a transcript of her first sitting and I was welcome to use it for the book if I wished. I said I would be glad to and we arranged for her to send it to me.

When Liz left to go home, she forgot to pay, as some sitters do, but this never worries me, for their happiness is truly more important. Liz was so elated with the results of her sitting that she simply forgot. An hour or so later, she phoned to apologise and I said there was no need to worry about it. Liz insisted, and two days later a parcel arrived on my doorstep. Inside I found a cheque, a card (which incidentally, Liz had hand-painted on to silk) and that beautiful water-colour of the fairy, which I now treasure among the many different pictures which cover the walls of my home.

The rest of Liz's story, as simple as it is, is explained in her own words:

I was as apprehensive of going to see Bryan as anyone else,

but perhaps for different reasons. I had been very aware of my father's presence since his death almost two years previously. So compelling had been the evidence of his survival that it had made me a convinced Spiritualist. So my apprehension was that Bryan would turn out to be what I consider one of those dreadful fortune tellers you see advertising in the personal columns of the newspaper. I couldn't have been more wrong! But first, I approached the matter with customary caution and went to "check him out" at a public display of clairvoyance at Lincoln Theatre Royale. It was very impressive to say the least and I listened to communications that I don't think I'll ever forget. One lady sat with growing discomfort next to an empty seat as Bryan tried in vain to connect a child who had passed over at two, with its parents. Unable to find anyone to claim the child, Bryan too was becoming a little desperate, for it was clearly important to the child to reach his parents. Eventually, the lady next to the empty seat spoke up, and in a shaky voice, admitted that the lady who should be in the empty seat next to her was the mother of the little child, and the details he had furnished about his parents and family were correct in every detail. There wasn't a dry eye in the house. The lady in the audience promised to ring the parents in the interval and indeed I saw her making an excited and emotional call as we queued for coffee.

Even so, it was almost five months later before I summoned up the courage to visit Bryan. If he should be unable to contact my family or had done so unconvincingly, it might have destroyed my own beliefs in the strange events since my father had died. Looking back, I feel how silly it was to have worried at all . . .

What follows is a selected transcript from a tape made at the time of the sitting. Where I have chosen to miss out a section, it is because the message was so personal as to be private, or it simply developed at greater length a point already established as correct. The readers will see I was doing my best to behave as a sitter should and trying hard not to give Bryan any clues or hints.

Bryan: (Talking about my still un-named father.) But when he left us, it was sudden, he's telling me. I know he was ill for a period, but he says, it was sudden. Can you understand it?
Liz: Yes, I . . . perhaps I can explain it to you later. It's

101

extremely . . . correct.

(Dad had been in hospital for six weeks having operations, first for cataracts and then unexpectedly for prostate problems. The second operation had revealed a slow and treatable cancer which, at Dad's age, should not have proved fatal. But he was frightened by the news and told no one. Concerned that he would become an invalid and dependent upon others, he quite simply decided to die. It is not a unique phenomena in my family. For a month, his biggest problem seemed to be depression and then quite suddenly he succumbed to pneumonia and died within forty-eight hours. Only the day before he died did I discover that he had been told he had cancer. I did not believe he had understood the doctor, for his hearing was poor on one side, so for two years I felt I had pushed him too hard in his recovery, since I too had no idea what was wrong. Bryan knew nothing of this.)

Bryan: That's what he says, because you see a lot of the time people didn't know what was wrong. Can you understand it? Because he was crafty, you see, and this is what he's trying to say to you in a way.

Liz: Did he know what was wrong?

Bryan: He knew what was wrong but other people didn't. Can you understand it?

Liz: Yes.

Bryan: And this is what your dad is trying to say to you, because you see, after he left, the family kind of felt, well . . . felt a bit uptight about things as if they should have seen more, or probably known a bit more. But as your father says, it was his choice and no-one else's, so you can accept that?

Liz: That helps.

Bryan: He knew what was wrong, he says . . . Right? But he felt he didn't want to worry other people.

Liz: Right.

Bryan: And the way he left us was quick, which was the way he wanted to go as well.

Liz: Yes.

Bryan: All right? He says, "I couldn't be an invalid. I couldn't be someone who had to depend on people."

Bryan: And Robert, can you understand Robert?

Liz: Oh, yes! (Robert or Bob is my husband.)

Bryan: Is that present-day?

Liz: That's present-day.

Bryan: Can you understand "self-employment" now?

(After dad died, we opened our own family engineering firm named in honour of my father. I, too, am self-employed as a freelance commercial artist.)

Liz: We have a family business.

Bryan: Does also the name Andrew mean anything, or was it Andrews as a surname?

Liz: It might be Andrews as a surname.

(Mrs. Andrews was a major and much-loved figure from my youth.)

Bryan: Right. So it is just your father says, "Well, I've just got to give Liz a few more . . . um . . . connections with him . . .

Liz: Yes.

Bryan: Well, he's trying his best . . . and John . . . can you understand John?

Liz: Oh, yes!

Bryan: In spirit?

Liz: That is him!

Bryan: He wants to give me a month now. Does February mean anything special at all?

Liz: That's when he died.

Bryan: He's giving me a name here and I don't know if this is past or present, because he hasn't given me any information; he's just given me a name. Does Dorothy mean anything to you?

(Dorothy is my sister who died suddenly and unexpectedly on my first birthday, aged one year eleven months. This was quite an emotional moment for me.)

Liz: That's my sister who is dead . . . can you tell me anything about her?

Bryan: With Dorothy – she has been up here a while.

Liz: Yes.

Bryan: Quite a long while; you didn't know a lot about her, did you? Because she was very young when she left us.

Liz: Yes.

Bryan: Well, he says "a babe" – can you understand me?

(Babe – rather than baby was a familiar expression of my father's.)

From there, Bryan went on to list accurately and without error the names of my other sister, her husband and son. In one and a half hours he gave me only five or six names that did not have strong associations close to the family. Some of these I have subsequently traced and shown to be correct through elderly friends and relatives. Only two still elude me and it is significant that these two names were the only two I could not accept at a sitting six months later. That later sitting became quite a family party, as Bryan named and described many of my family in spirit without error. Along came some much loved friends too, sometimes with messages for named members of their families which I have been able to pass on.

If one thing is clear from all this, it is this: Love is the most powerful force in the universe and the event we call "death" cannot separate us from our beloved.

ME DAD

"Me Dad" to me was special,
So big, so broad, and tall,
He lit my torch of happiness
And was around if I should fall.

He laid foundations for my life
And showed the way to me.
His heart was like the glistening Sun
So generous and kind was he.

"Me Dad" was not unusual,
He smoked, he drank, he swore!
His life was full and he worked hard,
To his loved ones, he gave all.

He worked down the pit, you know,
Came home, so wet and black.
But everyday he didn't forget
My much loved . . . ice-cream pack!

Oh, to me "Me Dad" was magic.
He'd dance you off the floor,
Then kiss and tuck you into bed
And gently close the door.

So, dear Lord, up in heaven,
If you've some time to spare,
Please tell "Me Dad" I love him so
And that I truly care.

By BRENDA GIBSON, Derby.

Chapter Twenty-two

THE INTERRUPTED SITTING

Spiritual work is often both serious and demanding, so it can be nice to look back occasionally at incidents which make us smile, even when, like this one, they were somewhat embarrassing at the time.

It was during November 1992, that this particular amusing episode took place. A nice couple named Pauline and Arnold arrived for a sitting and were welcomed with the usual cups of tea prior to starting the actual communication with spirit. Everything was going along quite smoothly until Pauline said to me, "Did you know that we have a visitor in the room?" Wondering what she was referring to, I turned to look and there, right in the middle of the carpet, sat a mouse who stared at us and then, as quickly as it had appeared, scurried off under the book shelves which were in front of the other door in the room. Neither Pauline nor Arnold seemed concerned and obviously were unafraid of mice, so I – trying to cover my embarrassment – said, "Perhaps it has come for a message," and as they laughed and said they were not worried about it being in the room, we continued with the sitting. However, a few minutes later, out came the mouse once more. I thought I would not be able to concentrate with all this going on so decided to find my cat, Poppy, who I knew was asleep upstairs.

Poppy was awakened much to her dislike and carried downstairs and pointed in the direction of where the mouse was situated. I even moved the shelves to expose the mouse, but Poppy was not interested and promptly turned tail, heading once more for bed. At this, the mouse decided to make a run for it across the carpet, under the other door into the kitchen, half-heartedly pursued by Poppy and myself. The mouse then seemed to run underneath the spin-dryer and disappear, so thinking that it had gone into the workings of the dryer, I decided to put it outside so that the mouse could escape into its natural environment as soon as it chose. Peace was once again restored, Poppy returned to her bed, and after I had apologised for the disturbance, the sitting was once more resumed.

As Pauline and Arnold left we laughed about the incident and Pauline hoped that the mouse had now left us and I would have no more unexpected visitors.

Although I remained very wary over the next few days, there did not seem to be any signs of the mouse and I could now relax with the sittings. I received a very nice letter from Pauline, thanking me for their sitting and saying how much they enjoyed the visit from the mouse, hoping that it had not made a return appearance.

I bumped into Pauline and Arnold when they came to see me at Retford Spiritualist Church, and once more the episode of the mouse was related to their friends, but then all thoughts of the mouse disappeared until April 1993, when the plumber came to see to the washing machine. On pulling out the machine, there all along the top were the trademarks of . . . yes, our mouse . . . and they were very much present-day ones as we had only had this machine a few weeks. The little terror was still with us and was obviously a very clever mouse, as it had not only evaded our detection but had run circles around Poppy over the last six months. This mouse certainly deserved to survive so, calling at the local pet shop, I purchased one of those mouse-traps which catch the mouse without killing it so that it can be released away from the home.

Everything was set in motion to capture our unwelcome guest. After a week of placing tempting food in the trap, nothing had happened and I was about to give up and accept that we would have our house-guest for evermore, until one morning I could hear this scratching going on. Eventually realising what it was, I saw that the little terror had finally been outwitted and it was ceremoniously taken right down to the bottom of the farm and released. Hopefully it has now joined up with its own family and is living a normal life in the natural environment.

Since this episode, the mouse-trap has remained, just in case, but so far it has had no takers.

I look forward to next meeting Pauline and Arnold, to bring them up to date with the information that at long last, the episode of the unwelcome guest at their sitting has been concluded, even though I shall probably continue to tell this story for many years to come.

Chapter Twenty-three

CATS, MORE CATS AND SPIRIT

About fifteen years ago, way before I was to become spiritually aware and work as a medium, whether coincidentally or not, I began to show an interest in cats. I collected anything associated with our feline friends. My vast collection now includes pictures, postcards and books relating to cats, and also over five-hundred cat ornaments which are spread all over the house – an enjoyable conversation piece with the many people who come to visit me. I am always delighted by the many sitters who send me a cat to add to the collection or by people arriving for a sitting who bring one with them in the hope that I have not got an identical one in my collection. Surprisingly, none are the same; some are similar but with different markings, and all of these very special cats have memories for me and some have interesting backgrounds and origins. People have asked if I collect cats because they are very spiritually-aware creatures, but at the beginning it was certainly not the reason. It is true that the Egyptians regarded the cat as part of their spiritual belief system and cats are very dominant in that culture.

Once at a get-together with friends in Kent, another medium was present at a sort of "open circle" and she explained that the Egyptian goddess of cats – Bast – was a strong link with me as a form of spiritual protection and I understood the meaning of this, knowing that this was yet another spiritual connection between myself and all cats.

Perhaps even at the beginning of collecting them, spirit was already preparing conditions for my later spiritual awareness. Having all these lovely cats around me not only gives me spiritual strength, but also gives spiritual warmth to my home and whoever enters it. Even my only real cat, "Poppy", sits happily amongst them and blends in with them; sometimes it is hard to know which is which, as many of the ornaments are as large as she is.

With all this around me, it is not surprising that in many different ways I would become more involved with our feline friends. When I lived in Bexley, I always had a cat, and on moving to my present home I was determined that I would not have another. However, after a year I was persuaded to take on two lovely kittens from the same litter; they were called Poppy and Timmy. They settled in and began to grow. At the time they were due to be neutered, Poppy decided that she wanted to be a mum, and eventually the family was enlarged to six; Timmy helped Poppy with the cleaning and control of the kittens. I had decided to keep one – a lovely ginger and white tom who would be known as Ginjar.

I was determined that Poppy and Timmy would get to see the vet and a date was booked. Sadly, the day before they were to go, Timmy was run over by a lady down the road – apparently not the first cat she had hit. So we lost a very missed member of our family. Homes had been found for the other three kittens and I was now looking after Poppy and Ginjar until a neighbour turned up with a little tabby kitten which they could not keep because of their dog, so it was included in the family and called Tiger Bay. Sadly, however, before it had reached its first birthday it was involved in a fight with a local stray tom-cat and due to its injuries died on the vet's operating table. A few weeks later, I lost Ginjar who wandered off one day never to return. So from that day I made up my mind – "No more cats, just Poppy" – and that is how it has stayed.

Mind you, I suppose I have weakened in a way as I have to admit to feeding a couple of cats who visit me each evening for their supper. Often they have to share it with a family of five hedgehogs who seem to rule them, because if the dish is empty the hedgehogs push it with their noses until it bangs against the door, demanding for it to be filled with their favourite cat food. Even Poppy has been known to share the same dish with them.

One of the cats I fed was a young, white tom-cat and very much a stray. No way could you get within ten feet of him; it took many months of gentle persuading and some very special treats before he would venture to the door, but we eventually became great friends. On a good night I would be honoured with being allowed to stroke him but at any sudden movement or noise he was off like a shot. As I did not know how to call him, I decided on the name "Snowy", and he began to recognise his new name and would come if called. However, more about Snowy later as, in his own right, he was to become a local celebrity and bring me into working much closer with the local Cat Protection League.

Regarding cats who leave for the spirit world, it still surprises me how people react when cats come through at a sitting wanting to be recognised. Many sitters can automatically accept that cats would come to let their friends know that they are all right, believing that animals as well as human-beings continue in the spirit world, but many people think that once their pet has left them then that is the end of the pet; how wrong they are.

We think of our pets, the animals we looked after, had contact with or helped unexpectedly – all animals who became part of our lives – and come to realise that they are also God's creatures who are treated no differently when they make that journey to the spirit world.

We talk to our pets, sometimes treating them better than we treat other members of our families. We tell them our secrets, spoil them and sometimes accuse them when there is no one else around to blame – and everyone of these creatures relates to us in different ways. Many times we hear people say that their pet listens to every word they say and answers them back in their own way. These very special pets are very much in tune to our thoughts and respond to our voices, holding a very important place in our lives, and when they leave us for the spirit world, for many of us it is the same as losing a member of the family. We mourn their passing as we do with our fellow beings; we make sure they are laid to rest in peace, often giving them their own special place in the garden where we can go and talk to them and have them near us. Some are given their own little tombstone with a special message on it. For many people these pets were often their only companion, their only family, and to them it is like losing a child.

So, my friends, why should there be any difference? These animals should be allowed the same chance as we have when we leave for the spirit world, and when the opportunity arises, to be able to come back to reassure us of their safe passage into the spirit world, so that we know they are at peace and no longer suffering, no matter how they departed. Many times, when that special pet comes through to us and communicates from spirit, they will impress upon us how they passed whether through accident, illness or old age. They understand the reasons they were taken to the vet's and did not return home, but they are at home with us in spirit.

How often I have received some very odd looks from the sitter when this happens and pets come through with such evidence to people who thought that when animals died that was the end of them. They still want to relate to us and their messages from spirit are translated into words which we can understand; the medium will be able to transmit them as evidence and the loyalty that the animal gave us will be there. Not only will there be confirmation of how they left for the spirit world, but hopefully the medium will be able to tell you the name they were called, maybe if you are lucky a precise description of what breed they were and perhaps any special colouring or markings which will convince their owners that it is really their own pet seeking to relate to them. I find that, like people in the spirit world, animals like to show their character, their temperament and their little individual ways of behaving, so that we are left in no doubt as to who they are. Perhaps the pet would go to work with its owner and travelled with them, and sometimes relate they are still with them, enjoying journeys – especially in lorries – even though they are now on a spiritual level and we cannot see them, but we often feel their presence around us.

Some pets even pass on messages regarding new pets who have joined the family in their place, remarking on how different they are to them, but knowing that they can never really be replaced because they have a unique place in their owner's heart.

Since working with spirit, I have linked with many different animals, not only cats but even horses and goldfish! Each one of these animals is special, and having been part of our life, always will be.

Chapter Twenty-four

SPECIAL PEOPLE AND CATS

At a very early stage of my spiritual work, I was determined to try to help the animal kingdom, and the only way I felt would be beneficial was to attempt to raise money for a charity. I suppose that given my link with cats, it was not surprising that I chose to help them.

I decided to contact the nearest branch of the Cat Protection League, which at the time was in Boston. They welcomed me aboard and shortly I took delivery of a collection box which was promptly placed on the table next to the chairs where people sat awaiting their sitting with me. It couldn't be missed, and as at that time I did quite a lot of healing which was a free service and many people wished to make a donation, this was the ideal charity as far as I was concerned. Over the next few years quite a healthy sum of money was to be collected and the box was often full within a few weeks, much to the delight of the organisation. Each time it was collected, I tried to build up a box of cat food as an extra bonus, especially as Poppy would go off certain brands as I had bought them, so into the box it would go as other cats would benefit from it and probably appreciate the food more than Poppy.

The marvellous people who devote much time and energy in caring for unwanted cats, take on the mammoth task of looking after them, travelling miles to collect them, have their homes invaded by strange cats, and having given them loving, tender care, make sure they are healthy. Then they have the tedious task of finding suitable homes for them and follow up their progress. It is all very time consuming. On top of this, there is fund-raising to meet vets' bills and to feed and house the cats. To me these are very special people and cannot be thanked enough.

Although I do not mind raising money for these animals, I never go to visit the places where they are housed, to see the cats. I know I would be too upset; it would make me feel very frustrated and I know I would want to keep them all. However, with my work and all the travelling I now do, it would be unfair on them. Hopefully, I may one day be in the position of having my own house with plenty of room, and enough time and money to help much more. There are many cats taken on by the Cat Protection League who will never be suitable to rehouse or who are too old to go through any more upheaval; these cats need that security.

All of my work with the Cat Protection League was done through a lovely lady named Betty and her husband, who lived at Kirton. We became good friends and then, two years ago, Betty suddenly left us for the spirit world, and I am sure, is now helping with those cats who arrive in spirit, giving them love and help. Since then, I have kept the box going, and last year, switched over to the Sleaford branch of the League which had just been formed. This came about through a sitter and my stray cat, Snowy, through whom I met a lady named Hazel Pawley, her daughter, Sue, and their family and friends who work so tirelessly to help these very special creatures.

In 1992, a lady came to see me for a sitting. We talked about cats and I mentioned that I would do anything to raise funds for them. A few weeks later, I received a phone call from her asking if I would be willing to visit her home to give a talk and demonstration as she was inviting a few people around and would give the proceeds to the Cat Protection League; she had got a lovely cat from them and this would be a way of thanking them. The event was arranged at her house in North Kyme for 19th November, 1992, and when I arrived the house was full; how she managed to get nearly fifty people in there amazed me. Our local vicar and his wife also came along to give support and kindly gave me a lift there. The whole evening was a great success and everybody enjoyed themselves. A raffle was held and the evening resulted in over £300 being raised which certainly helped a few more cats. It was on that evening I came into contact with Hazel and Sue who were thrilled with the event, and I offered to do another for them any time. As we were talking, a strange coincidence happened, as we found that we both had a mutual interest in a tom-cat called "Snowy", who Sue now had at her home and had christened "Henry", so I can now unfold the story of Snowy/Henry.

You will remember that Snowy had arrived as a stray at my home, eventually becoming more trusting, coming some mornings as well as evenings for food. He would spend hours lying on the bonnet of my car between disappearances; no matter what time I came home, Snowy would be there. Unfortunately, my cat Poppy did not like Snowy and would hiss and growl at him, but Snowy would just ignore her, hold his ground and continue eating. Occasionally another cat who came for food (this one a neighbour's cat) would join Snowy and they would eat together. Later on, I found out that this cat called "Fluff" was actually Snowy's mother and they still related to each other. Although I made enquiries, nobody seemed to own Snowy and it appeared that he often visited other people for food. As Snowy was obviously still quite young and looked quite mangy and not very white at the time, I was tempted to take him to the vet to be neutered, but never actually got around to doing so.

By now Snowy was a regular, and not a day went by without him making an appearance; I had got used to him being there. In the autumn 1992 Snowy disappeared, and after a couple of days I thought he must have found a better home. It was not until the morning of the third day that I received a phone call from a lady named Kate who knew me. She lived the other side of the village. She asked me whether I owned a white cat as she had seen one at my house, but I replied, "It's not mine. I do feed it, but it's a stray." Kate then went on to say that it had been run over in the early hours of the morning near her home and it was at the vet's, and she thought I should know. I promptly contacted the vet to check if it was Snowy, and sure enough, it was. I was told that he had three broken legs, and on top of that, was feeling very sorry for himself as he had been neutered at the same time. I explained about Snowy and that I didn't own him but was willing to meet any bills for his treatment, to which they replied that the bills had already been taken care of by the Cat Protection League who were also going to find a home for him. Sadly, I decided that I should not claim him because of my own cat Poppy and her dislike for Snowy, but as long as he had a home to go to, I was happy and thought that was the end of my contact with him.

Then, a few weeks later, who should be on the front page of the local paper? Yes – Snowy, with his picture and the story of his amazing escape and recovery. As I found out the night I met Hazel and Sue, they had Snowy (now known as Henry) and in their capable hands he was doing well, although he was still very wary of people. We swapped stories, but that was not the end. There was a sequel to the story of this amazing cat, which left a lasting reminder of his presence at my home.

From the 'Sleaford Own Independent Newspaper'.

You may recall that several issues ago we brought you the story of the remarkable recovery being made by 'Henry' the cat after he had been hit by a vehicle at Kirby la Thorpe and left for dead.

Well, not only is Henry continuing to make fine progress after his ordeal, in which he sustained three broken legs, but his saga has an added chapter.

Recently seven kittens have been discovered which are believed to be the offspring of Henry and bear testament to the fact that prior to his accident he liked to enjoy a healthy social life. Two of the kittens, are all white, just like their dad.

Henry and the kittens are currently in the care of the Sleaford Cat Protection League.

Unknown to us all, just before his accident, Snowy had mated with Fluff, and a few weeks after all the publicity, Fluff produced seven beautiful kittens, two being pure white just like Snowy. As I was still feeding Fluff following Snowy's departure, I was aware of the situation. Fluff's owner was elderly and his daughter was a friend of mine, so I contacted her to ask if she knew the cat had had kittens. She replied, "Yes. I expect I shall have to find homes for them again." She thought Fluff had been doctored after the previous litter as she was quite old, but had relied on her sister who lived close to their father to arrange everything. I explained to Jackie about the people in the Cat Protection League who would find good homes for the kittens and also have Fluff doctored at no charge to her father. She promised to speak to her father and get back to me, which she did. It was all arranged for this to be done, and Fluff has now been doctored, the kittens all have good homes, and once more Snowy was front-page news, this time with a photograph of him with all seven kittens to go with the story. Fluff is fine and still comes around for her food. Henry has come out of his shell and mixes with people, still walking a little awkwardly after the accident, but enjoying being a permanent resident with Sue.

It is strange how this all came about. I am now more involved with the Cat Protection League and on 27th April, 1993, we held a large demonstration at the Lincolnshire Oak. Every ticket was sold way before the night, and once more, a successful evening was held not only for the cats' fund as over £500 was raised, but also for spirit. Many people who had never experienced the work of spirit were given the chance to understand something of our work and now wish to have private sittings, so good has been achieved all round. I look forward to being able to do more fund-raising evenings for those special people who continue to give their time and love to help these very remarkable creatures who, through no fault of their own, are neglected, abandoned and unloved, but spirit cares for them and will protect them.

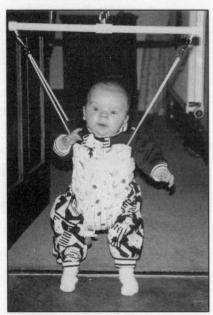

Young Jack.

My friend Tony.

Liz Butterfield's dad and son Chris.

Card about the interrupted sitting.

Cat Protection League at Lincolnshire, Oak Sleaford.

Henry (Snowy).

117

Fluff (Henry's mum).

Daisy the hen.

Brownlow.

Chapter Twenty-five

MEMORIES OF GERT AND DAISY

Some of you will already have heard of Gert and Daisy – two hens who shared our family life up to a few years ago. They had lived originally on the farm with the other hens and bantams but managed to outlive all the others by between two or three years.

They were real characters, often eating Poppy's cat food before she managed it herself, and sharing her mat in the hallway, enjoying perfectly friendly relations, except when they had the occasional urge to give her a peck.

Even after they stopped producing eggs, the two would routinely sit on the nest each day, hoping for better results. They were just like sisters, following Poppy or me around, and were always together. Visitors who came for sittings became used to their antics, although some looked startled to have to avoid the odd "whoopsie" on their mat. I didn't mind clearing up after them, but I suppose some people found it somewhat unhygienic!

One night Gertie died in her sleep, and I found her the next morning looking perfectly peaceful in the nest-box. She had had a good life and a natural death, but now Daisy had to do without her. Gradually Daisy became more dominant and enjoyed a closer bond with Poppy, sharing her food, and the two of them followed me around wherever I went. Poppy would sometimes tease her and Daisy would amuse onlookers by flapping her wings and pecking Poppy if she forgot her good manners too much.

Daisy was very much part of our family and people would ask after her just as much as anybody else. She looked sprightly and young even when she wasn't and nobody really thought about the fact that one day she too would leave us.

Sadly, the time came when I noticed that Daisy was losing her sense of direction and seemed to be having difficulty in seeing. When I came home one night I found her sitting in the middle of the drive instead of in the shed where she slept at night, and I had to put her to bed.

She did not arrive on the door-step the next morning for her food, and it was obvious that she was now totally blind and could only eat if I helped her. I gave a lot of thought about what best to do for Daisy to lessen her suffering and whether I should continue to feed her myself, but spirit enabled me to see that this would not be natural for Daisy. Eventually I contacted the farmer to arrange for her to be put out of her distress. It was very sad to lose her as she had made me laugh and was a valued part of our lives but I knew that she and Gertie would be able to be free to enjoy themselves in the spirit world. They are often in my thoughts and I have seen them since in the house. They frequently come into the hall just as they did previously, walk around and then go out again, as if to say, thanks. We are still part of each others' lives.

Where animals are treated with love and kindness by us, they can and do come back to reassure us of their continued existence and always give us back the love we shared with them.

Chapter Twenty-six

MORE ANIMALS IN SPIRIT – BROWNLOW

In my previous books, I have mentioned "Brownlow", a cow who made a great impact on my life some time ago. I should like to remind you of her story, as so often people think that only human beings are of importance on this earth and that when the time comes for animals to die, that is the end of them. The truth is, animals are made of the same divine energy which gives us life and deserve our respect and love just as much as our "two-legged" friends and relatives.

For as long as I have lived on the farm, cows have always been brought in for the winter and housed in the crew-yard. Until then, I had had nothing to do with farm animals and getting to know them was a new experience for me. When I became involved with looking after them (as a favour to Tom, the farmer), it all came very easily and naturally as if I had done it before. How far this was due to the knowledge and experience of my guide, Running Foot, and how much was due to any of my previous life experiences, I am not sure, but whatever the reason, the animals always seemed to be calm and responsive to my being around them. Over the years, I would get used to their return each winter, even after they had got older and had calves of their own, and each year they would respond to the sound of my voice; I got to know some of them very well indeed.

One winter, they were affected by a virus and I saw many of these beautiful creatures sicken before leaving for the spirit world. I spent many hours giving them healing, often staying with them in the crew-yard, talking to them and trying to comfort them until their time here on earth came to an end. I hated the thought of their being alone and untended, having no one to reassure them in their sickness and distress. To me each one was special and I really wanted them to have a peaceful transition into the spirit world.

The most special of them all to me was named "Brownlow", who I had known as a calf, the only brown and white one among them. She was always the most gentle and affectionate and we had, it seemed, a special bond between us. We understood each other and she remained just as soft and affectionate even when she had been away for her regular summer holidays in the meadow. Eventually Brownlow produced her own calf, brown and white like herself. They were brought back for the winter to the crew-yard and housed there with the other cows. She was pleased to see me, but this time something was different. She seemed unwell and I tried to feed her separately as she appeared anxious and waited until all the others had eaten before she would attempt to eat. The farmer took little notice and I eventually took it upon myself to separate Brownlow and her son by themselves so that they would not be bothered by the others with whom she seemed so nervous. It was obvious that Brownlow was becoming weaker and unable to feed her calf adequately. The farmer said nothing could be done and the calf would have to be bottle-fed, declining to seek help from the vet. ·

It was Christmas and I spent most of it sitting in the yard cradling Brownlow's head and talking to her. She would look at me with those beautiful eyes as if to say, "Thank you". By now, Brownlow's son was unable to stand and would just lie beside her trying with difficulty to feed from the bottle. On Boxing Day, the calf gave a long sigh as I was cradling it, and with the bottle still in its mouth, left for the spirit world. It was a very sad moment. I felt so helpless, and could only try to reassure Brownlow that her calf was no longer suffering and I believe she understood. They were not my animals and I had no say in what happened to them, but I felt so powerless as I watched Brownlow become weaker. She seemed to have given up her right to live, and I knew that soon she would be with her son. At this late stage, the farmer did decide to arrange for someone to come and humanely put Brownlow out of her discomfort. I just wished it had been possible for me to have done more for them.

To many people, cows and other such creatures represent only money. To others of us these animals are loved in their own right. What little help and comfort we can provide for them in their short and sometimes sad lives is, I think, of great importance.

Chapter Twenty-seven

SPAIN, THE FIRST TIME

I have been told by many other mediums, ever since the very beginning of my spiritual development, that they could see me working abroad. They usually mentioned America which always sounded nice, but throughout the first six years of my working as a medium, nothing of the sort transpired.

Whenever anyone has asked me whether I have worked abroad, my answer has always been that if ever I were lucky enough to do so, it would be because others had invited me on the strength of my work as a medium. Those spiritually-aware people and mediums who are in the position of having unlimited funds to travel around the world, do become well known as others get to know of their gift, which obviously increases their work beneficially to them, but hopefully also spreads the word of spirit a little further afield.

Rightly or wrongly, I have always believed that if I am meant to work in another country, then spirit will create the situation, or arrange for the right people to contact me through having seen me demonstrate. Obviously, the thought of travelling and working abroad sounds very exciting. I am no different from many others and can let my imagination work overtime. Naturally, the places we tend to picture in our mind are usually the more exotic countries. I am sure most mediums would not say "no" to having the chance to visit such countries as America or Australia, for instance.

Imagine my surprise when I was given the chance of working abroad. It never entered my head that it would be Spain, especially as it is such a religious country. It has always been one of the places which I have said many times I never wanted to visit, even on holiday, but it seems that spirit had other ideas and felt that this was a good initiation in working abroad.

The connection with Spain came about through a lady named Marie Louise. The invitation developed from a sitting in July 1992. Marie Louise, who originally came from Belgium, had recently lost her husband

and at that time needed to know he was at peace. The sitting was being taped and it appears that everything related from her husband was very accurate and positive. Having thought no more about this situation, a few weeks later I received a very nice letter from Marie Louise, thanking me for the sitting and the help it had given her, and saying that now she could get on with the rest of her life. Three months later, I received a letter from Spain. I was very surprised to find that it was from a lady called Johanna Keen, living in Spain, telling me that she had heard the tape which her mother (Marie Louise) had sent her. She was very impressed and wondered whether she could arrange a visit for me to Spain. She offered to pay my expenses and arrange a possible demonstration, as she knew many people wanted private sittings, having talked about it within her community. Strangely, I did not have to consider it for long as I felt it was right, and was able to reply promptly to Johanna, giving possible dates in 1993.

A date was fixed for March 1993, with Johanna arranging accommodation for us. It was agreed that any surplus money made at the demonstration, and charity auction following it, would be given to a Christian children's charity. This gave Johanna six months for the organisation of all the details. It was expected that the majority of the people attending would be British, but with a few Spanish people attending, an interpreter would be available. We sent information and posters and left everything in Johanna's capable hands.

I had help with this new venture and would not be travelling alone. John Brett, a close friend and very talented psychic artist had agreed to work with me, which would not only enable him to gain further experience but would be an extra bonus for the people in Spain who had probably never before seen a psychic artist work.

The months up to March soon passed. We were booked to fly out to Spain on 27th February, 1993, and arrived at Alicante airport on a very cold, wet and windy Saturday morning, where we were met by our hosts, Johanna and Ray Keen. They were lovely people who made us feel at home straightaway. It was as if we had known them for years and they certainly made me feel at ease.

It was quite a long drive from the airport to our destination, Torrevieja, where Johanna had managed to secure for us a lovely, spacious villa which overlooked a valley of trees alongside the local golf course. It was quiet, the fridge was full and we were left to settle in. The weather worsened and a thunderstorm very quickly arrived which caused the electricity to fail. We were left in the dark and John went to the local store to buy some candles. While he was gone, I managed to locate the fuse box, and on John's return the lights came on again when he flicked the switch. I was beginning to wonder what I had let myself in for. I had been told how nice and warm it was going to be, but now everyone was apologising for the weather, which continued for the next couple of days. I joked to myself that some people might think it was my fault and that it was a message from spirit.

The demonstration was arranged for the Saturday and Johanna had booked some private sittings in the days leading up to it. She was a little upset as a number had backed out with various excuses, but I didn't mind, thinking I would have some time to relax. However, this did not materialise as the first two days proved to be full up with sittings. Johanna said there were only one or two to do over the next few days, but as the word spread and people heard about the sittings that had already taken place, they came knocking on the door asking if they could book, so in the end I worked every day except for the day of the demonstration, which ended with a midnight supper to which everyone had contributed.

The venue for the demonstration had been offered free of charge in the "Stables Bar", owned by a Spanish gentleman and run by an English couple. It had been agreed with the managers that no drinks would be served during the demonstration and that after 10 p.m., business would go on as normal. It appears that in Spain it is usual to leave everything until the last minute, and although quite a few tickets had been sold, no one knew how many to expect. Johanna was therefore expecting a few minor hiccups and near the time was getting a little frustrated to find that the couple who ran the bar had not arranged any food for the midnight supper, which in the end had to be cancelled. However, the demonstration and charity auction were still to take place.

When John and I arrived about ten minutes before the beginning of the demonstration, attendance seemed quite good and others were still arriving. There was a gentleman present who would interpret if required for the only two Spanish ladies who were there. I was introduced by a lovely lady called Marie and proceeded to tell them a little about my work and what they could expect to happen, explaining what I needed from them in terms of their answering me and confirming that they understood the messages. The atmosphere was very friendly and spiritual. I was looking forward to telling Johanna that having done such a lot of private sittings, all my expenses had been covered and all money taken that night could now go to the children's charity.

Johanna had also arranged for the demonstration to be recorded on video as a nice memento of our first visit to Spain. Everything got off to a good start with a very positive message and very up-to-date information following. At this point, a gentleman called Eddie wanted to talk to quite a few in the room, telling them of his tragic accident and apologised to those who had paid for work to be done and lost out. This seemed to stun them for a while but the mood soon switched when I went to a dear lady named Margaret who would not admit to being very deaf and insisted that she could understand me. Two ladies sitting nearby repeated the messages to her as I asked her if she could accept a gentleman called Bill, who wished to talk to her. She said in a rather loud and surprised voice, "Good God, I'd forgotten all about him!" He proved only to be her second husband. He proceeded to give her evidence of the family, also mentioning the name "John" in the family, to which she said "no", until reminded by those near her that it was her son John he was talking about as she had been worried about him. She was pleased about this and certainly caused a lot of merriment with those around her. She certainly lifted the atmosphere and was one of the stars that night.

The demonstration had been in progress for almost two hours with good evidence being accepted. Then sadly the mood changed once more. Unknown to me, the bar had been kept open and drinks had been flowing; mostly with a crowd of about ten people who had all been standing behind the bar. One gentleman was gradually becoming rather loud, and when I went to a lady near him with information regarding a lady named Lilian and her husband, Arthur, which she could accept and place, this rather aggressive man insisted that the message was for him. He said his father was called Arthur and that he had been waiting all night for a message, wanting me there and then to relate to him. I politely said that if the message was for him, then I would try to come back to him later, wanting to complete the message I had already started to pass on to the lady. Being told to "shut up" by other people only made him worse. (I was told later that his alcoholism was well known.) However, I decided to plod on and managed to deliver two more positive messages in spite of the increasing noise from behind the bar, which was getting past a joke. Because the time had gone 10 p.m., reluctantly I brought the evening to a close, thanking everyone for their support and thinking to myself, "Well, that certainly was an experience, but spirit was strong and the messages were correct and accepted."

Another gentleman asked me about my guide, Running Foot, querying what tribe he belonged to, which I answered. He then asked whether I believed that Running Foot was communicating with me, to which I replied, "Of course." He exclaimed, "That's a load of rubbish!" saying that he knew all about Indians and had worked with them, and that no Indian would ever talk through or help a white man. Once again, I politely answered that I was sorry, but I know who works with me, and the gentleman was perfectly free to believe what he wanted, leaving it at that.

At this stage, I was unaware that Johanna had gone home. Apparently she was so upset at what was happening at the bar, to control herself she left for home. Whilst I was talking to those who had received messages, quite a scuffle appeared to break out at the bar and someone was removed outside. Apparently it was not unusual for fights to break out there, and one had to be defused involving the man who had caused most of the trouble. After this, people settled down and started talking again.

John's pictures had been accepted, and people were thanking us for coming and enquiring about further private sittings. However, as I had only two days left, not much more was possible. Because of the trouble, many people had gone home and the gentleman in charge of auctioning the items decided it would be advisable to hold the auction at a later date. In spite of the fiasco, I still felt John and I had brought the work of spirit to Spain and been able to pass the messages to those who needed them.

When we all got back to a tearful Johanna, we reassured her that in spite of the problems, the evening had been a success. I had enjoyed the challenge and told her that working with spirit is not always easy, adding that we hoped we would be asked to come again. This was quickly agreed by Johanna and the next visit is arranged for the autumn, hopefully in a venue without a bar where we can avoid some of the pitfalls we previously experienced.

Although I did not know what to expect when I agreed to accept the invitation, my visit to Spain certainly will not be forgotten. I am sure I have learned a lot from the experience, although working abroad is not really so very different from working at home. People are still the same in that they wish for communication with their loved ones, both family and friends in spirit.

It was also a pleasure to discover that so many people there are very spiritually aware, many of them commenting that they missed the opportunity to visit churches and meetings in England and wished somewhere local was available. One of the ladies who came for a private sitting is now hoping to form a group locally, although people there have in the past kept their spiritual beliefs to themselves, and it may now be possible for them to be more open about things.

If our visit to Spain has helped a few to understand what spirit is about, then it was worthwhile. Now we look forward to planning our next trip and the adventures which lie ahead.

Extract from a newspaper article.

THE WORLD OF SPIRIT
by Anita Bond

For us living beings, death has a finality about it that's frustratingly painful. Our loved ones who have died and left us are reduced to just a memory, lost to us for ever. Or are they?

There are those who claim to have a link to the other side; those who see death as just a passing over of that thin line between one life, as we know it, and another form of life. Such a person is called a medium.

My curiosity in these matters is great. It was, therefore, with a mixture of excitement, scepticism and rationalism, that I went for a sitting with a medium, Bryan Gibson, who was visiting Torrevieja recently from Sleaford, Lincolnshire.

Before I give you an account of my sitting, I will have to tell you something about myself.

Some ten months ago, my little dog, Napoleon, died during a run-of the mill castration operation.

Not having children, my love for this animal was great; as was his for me.

As many of you can imagine, I was devastated when told of his unexpected and untimely death.

I had been the one who had made the decision to have him castrated, been the one to bring him to the vet's, and told him, "Off you go, darling. You'll be all right."

It was the first time I had left him alone. Other operations and treatments he had needed had always been done in my presence.

Besides my grief, you may be able to understand my guilt feelings which have rested heavily upon my heart since his death.

When I read in Bryan's books, *Just A Touch Away* and *I Am Here Listening*, that the spirits of animals also come through to him, it seemed like a golden opportunity for me to make amends.

I'd also had a powerfully strong love for my father like, I must add, most daughters have for their fathers.

But Dad has been dead for twenty-two years now; time to get used to him being gone.

With these two factors locked in my psyche. I went to meet the man who could maybe get in touch with their spirits.

Bryan Gibson is a pleasant looking person. He has a relaxed manner about him and none of the special effects so often associated with those who claim to be one step ahead of us non-gifted mortals.

First, Bryan explained that I was not to offer him any information whatsoever.

He would tell me things which the spirit world were saying to him, and I was only to inform him if these things made any sense to me.

He was just switching the tape recorder on when, without any wailing of "Is there anyone there?" Bryan asked me if

October meant anything to me. Yes, it did. (My Dad's birthday.)

A gentleman had come through, Bryan told me, who was talking ten to the dozen and so fast he could hardly understand him.

This man was fighting to get through and kept elbowing a couple of other spirits out of the way in his determination to be heard.

Then Bryan threw out a few names. Charles? Did this mean something?

A young lady interrupted; she died of cancer, not a family member but our earthly emotional relationship was equal to her being a sister.

(Sheila! Died, aged thirty-five, from cancer of the bowel just six years ago.)

That man wouldn't stop talking though. Did I know a William? Bill, maybe? And it seemed there was a John here. (I don't have or had friends of these names.)

"And someone called Robert . . . it's all quite confusing," Bryan said.

"Shut up!" Bryan finally told the spirit. "You are getting too much for me."

Bryan rubbed his chest and informed me he was having difficulty breathing.

The spirit with whom he was in contact had trouble with his chest in life, although he didn't die of a chest problems.

Rather his demise was caused by a number of ailments for which he was in hospital for some weeks.

"When this gentleman finally passed over, it came as a surprise because doctors and family alike thought he was on the road to recovery.

"He's smiling ironically and telling me that he wasn't very old though," continued Bryan. Tears sprang to my eyes.

My father was known to me all of my life as Robert Bond. He'd taken the name 'Bob' shortly after the war while singing semi-professionally on the Midlands club circuit because there was already a 'Charlie Bond' doing the rounds.

My father's real name was Charles John William Bond!

The spirit, who by this time I was firmly convinced was really father, then went on to reminisce about old times when I, young as I was, would accompany him to the pub that he worked in.

These were things that lay some thirty to forty years back in time.

"I see him in uniform. The R.A.F., I think," said Bryan. "No," I said. "Yes," insisted Bryan. "Definitely something to do with planes.

"Was he a pilot?" (No, he wasn't.) "Can I give you information?" I offer Bryan. "No! But spirit is adamant that he had something to do with planes."

Bryan moved on and I was left harbouring the knowledge that my father was, during the war, a paratrooper who remained a faithful member of the association for the rest of his life

For the following hour and a half, Bryan kept throwing information at me which I felt sure he couldn't have gleaned from my simple presence.

Of one thing I am sure: Bryan is not telepathic. During the whole session, I was concentrating the wish for Napoleon to make contact. Bryan never picked this up.

The rest of the sitting was filled with astounding facts.

Eighty per cent of what he said hit the nail right on the head, and this included the information pertaining to 'He Who Should Be Obeyed' who was sitting beside me and was contacted by his, unknown to him in life, grandmother.

This would mean that spirit has no language barriers, for my other half is German.

Bryan described the character traits, even the not-so-nice ones, of his spiritual subjects very accurately.

It seemed like the session was winding up to a close. My father had settled down, happy now that I knew he was just a touch away, waiting for me.

He'd let Mam have her say and even made room for my partner's side to come through.

"Was that it?" I asked, disappointment apparent in my voice. "'Isn't there anyone, anything else?"

"Just a second," admonished Bryan. "We are coming to animals now."

Did I have a cat? "No," I answered. Looking back, the disappointment must have been written clearly on my face.

"Your mother is holding a cat," Bryan went on. Clouded memories of Skipper, my fat tortoise-shell tom-cat who accompanied me through my childhood came drifting back.

"There's a spaniel here too, wagging his tail. You had to have him put to sleep."

My face lights up as I think of Bruno, my English Springer Spaniel who, sadly, had to be put to sleep due to illness when he was eight.

I was so obviously waiting for something else. It was written in my gestures, in my body language of leaning forward, in the hopefulness upon my face.

I sat back. I'm giving off too much information, I admonished myself.

"He shouldn't have died, he's telling me," said Bryan. "He didn't have an accident though. I feel pain in his throat and upper chest." I answered no.

"Yes," Bryan was sure. "He was having an operation. But not one he needed. Was he being doctored?"

"Yes," I managed to squeak out while blowing my nose. "He died from the anaesthetic," said Bryan. "He tells me to tell you he is all right now." But I'm not. I weep.

During the sitting, John Brett had been quietly sketching. He was not facing either myself or my partner.

One picture he had drawn, from my side of the family, was unrecognisable to me, but then I never knew any grandparents.

The other picture was, to my eyes, a remarkable likeness of my partner's mother.

On reflection, and to summarise, the sitting was a most unusual experience.

Bryan Gibson most definitely has something special that is not to be found in most of us. His apparent contact to something or someplace, that is denied to the majority of us, is very realistic and convincing.

Whereas he may be playing some type of complicated guessing game with the people who seek comfort through him, I feel his motives are good and genuine.

He knew things about my parents and past that even my partner doesn't know although I bombard him with information about myself and childhood daily.

I think I believe that I have had, through Bryan, contact with the spirit world.

This feeling will diminish daily, I suspect, until, in a few months' time my logical scepticism will take over, cloud the memory and return me to the world of the 'Well, I'm not quite convinced'.

Of one thing though I am certain; when Bryan returns to Spain, I shall be one of the first to book another sitting with this remarkable medium.

Chapter Twenty-eight

THE SPIRITUALIST ASSOCIATION OF GREAT BRITAIN

In my seven short years as a working medium, I have been very lucky. I have been given the chance to achieve many things, especially spiritually; not just to further my own spiritual progress, but also to meet lots of different people from many countries and various walks of life. Each new episode of my spiritual ladder has proved challenging and progressive and has given me the chance to present spirit more effectively – not just to those people who are already spiritually aware, but also to those who are seeking to become so, those who themselves doubt how spirit work, and those who do not know of the help and guidance available from our loved ones in spirit who wish to come to reassure us of their love and contentment in their new spirit home.

Since the beginning of my spiritual ladder was so sudden without any circle development or other earth-level influences, I was very fortunate to have very strong spirit communicators who had faith in my ability to work with them and to allow me to progress naturally, learning from my own mistakes. They knew I would take note and correct my spirit work to get the best communication from the many spirit communicators with whom I would come into contact.

We all have to start at the beginning of anything, and I was lucky to be presented with the opportunity to serve the spiritualist church at Sleaford who had heard of my sudden awareness of spirit although they had not seen me work. This was followed by an invitation to give talks and demonstrate my gift to small groups of people – mainly Ladies' Circles, W.I. meetings and Young Farmers' Clubs, which were certainly a challenge. I had not had any experience of public speaking but certainly learned a lot in a short space of time. The work was certainly expanding and it moved into larger demonstrations in halls to raise money for charities, many of which I now support on a regular basis. It often happened that those attending these meetings were spiritually unaware, which would stretch me even further and naturally strengthen my gift a little more. Eventually the next step arose, which was to spread the word of spirit by working with a much larger number of people in theatres. This meant reaching out to those who had never seen a medium work before, many of them having just come along to "take the mickey", and who were often surprised with a message from their loved ones in spirit. Each one of these episodes has opened doors, enabling me to go and work further afield.

In 1992, I was invited to give a demonstration for Newark Spiritualist Church at their meeting place in the Scout Hall, Lovers Lane, Newark, to help to raise money for the church. The evening was very well attended and communications with spirit were well accepted. After the demonstration, I was approached by a lady who said that her sister-in-law was the President of the Spiritualist Association of Great Britain (S.A.G.B.) in Belgrave Square, London, and asked if I would agree to my name being recommended to the lady in question, as she felt they could benefit from my kind of mediumship. Obviously I was very pleased to have been approached with such a request and gave my address and telephone number, wondering when and if I would ever hear anything more about it.

It was not until six months later that I received a letter from Jenny Ahmed, asking me whether I would consider accepting a booking for the S.A.G.B. and asking for dates when I was available.

I was able to give more time to concentrate on my work as John Brett had become my manager, taking the stress off me. John is a very talented psychic artist and we thought it would be nice for us to have a go at working together as we had done occasionally at various churches. Jenny agreed to this suggestion, and before we knew it we had been invited to the S.A.G.B. for July 1993, to work over a four-day period giving private sittings and public demonstrations.

I must admit to having been a little apprehensive but excited at the new challenge. Once again this was meant to be, as I had been told that to work at the S.A.G.B., you had to go there to demonstrate in order for the committee to pass your mediumship as being up to the required standard, but here we were being taken on recommendation, so spirit had to be confident that we would represent them correctly.

We were welcomed on our arrival at the S.A.G.B. and shown to quarters which would be home to us for the next four days. As newcomers, it was difficult to know how we would be received by the other mediums working there. We need not have worried. The two ladies staying there were very helpful and friendly, giving us all the information we needed as to where everything was. Soon it was time to start work and we were allocated a room for the sittings and a list of times of sittings. We set everything up, such as the tape recorder and John's table for his drawings, and waited. All the sittings had been booked up before we arrived which was unusual as we were not known mediums, but it appears that some people had read my books and booked on the strength of them.

As the first sitter did not turn up, I didn't feel this was a very promising start, but everyone else arrived and we had no more problems. I was concerned that our first demonstration that evening would be all right. I knew John Thorpe who had been responsible for publishing my books would be there and didn't want to let him down. He had arranged for my books to be on display with a large poster.

The evening was better attended than I expected. On the few occasions when I had visited the S.A.G.B. to attend a demonstration, there had only been a handful of people present apart from when Coral Polge, the well-known psychic artist was working, but we had managed to attract over fifty people. The evening was very positive, and the messages were accepted and John's drawings found homes, so the weekend passed quickly. The Saturday was especially hectic as we had to go straight from the last sitting into the demonstration without even time for a drink, but once again it was enjoyable. Other mediums commented, "If you can work here, you can work anywhere", and I now agree with them.

All of the work at the S.A.G.B. was very demanding, not least when the first sitter proved to be a German lady who spoke hardly any English. Luckily, she had a young lady with her to interpret, which I found frustrating at first, since it was sometimes difficult to keep the flow going whilst the communication was relaying from her husband and brother in spirit had to be interpreted into German and her following reply translated into English. However, as usual, spirit coped and the messages were successfully passed on.

The rest of the afternoon just flew by and soon it was time to pack our bags for the return journey. However, we were lucky in being able to book a sitting with Coral Polge for the following day, which was a special treat for me. What a wonderful person she proved to be. She drew two of my guides for me, and as she had attended one of our demonstrations, was very helpful in offering John some positive advice with his drawings, so our visit to London ended well. I really felt that the challenge and change of scenery had given me renewed inspiration with my own spiritual progression and I look forward to the new challenges which come my way. I am glad to say we expect to be returning to the S.A.G.B. and to fix more dates with them for future visits. My visit to London seems to have given me a boost, knowing that wherever I go spirit are always there with me and never letting me down. I hope that I never let spirit down and continue to work to the best of my ability, helping those who need help and showing that our loved ones who make that journey to their second home – Spirit – are at peace, still listening to our voices, watching over us, and giving us their love and strength when needed.

LILAC TREE – MOTHER TREE

I stand within your garden
Through wind, rain, frost and snow
Awaiting for the breath of spring
For life within to grow,
Then long awaited baby buds
Their heads begin to show.

One by one by leaves unfurl.
I watch my children play
As they swing and dance and jump about
On a warm and breezy day.

Joy of joy,
Fullness of heart,
My flowers open wide.
The lilac cones in such array
Make tears of gladness start.

A fragrance sweet as slumber
On a sunny afternoon –
Take it, share it, will you?
This is my gift to you.

Some people say my children
Are portents of doom, and
As they pass they rip and crush
My delicate soft blooms.
How my heart weeps silently;
How could they be so cruel.

On broken bough my leaves turn brown
Unsightly to the eye,
But that limb was a part of me, and
As each day goes by
Like tear drops all my leaves descend
And my cones have all gone dry.

When I saw you with tear-stained face,
With seeing, yet unseeing eyes,
I felt your anger and your pain
And heard your questions, "Why?"
Your ears were closed to answers.
Mechanically you walked away,
For the only answer I can give is
"Spring will come again".

As you see me relentlessly,
Through wind, rain, frost and snow
Awaiting for the breath of Spring
For my baby buds to grow.

For my branches they reached out to you
In your bitter, deep despair,
But you did not notice me –
How could you? – standing there.
Your eyes were cloudy and tear-filled
For you had lost your baby bud
And your soul felt killed.

Just like when my heart bleeds,
You know I'm alive like you.
For you are a mother of children
And I am a mother of blooms.

PAUL D. UNDERWOOD

Chapter Twenty-nine

A NUDGE FROM SPIRIT

Life moves on and always provides new opportunities for service, but readers of my earlier books may remember how I talked about a gentleman named Bernard.

Bernard had booked a sitting with me and on his arrival was hoping for a link with his family and friends in the world of spirit, but also hoping for guidance with a work situation which was bothering him. Bernard accepted his family's names and messages and confirmed the correctness of names given of present-day members of the family. Spirit continued to prove their knowledge about his life, stating that he wore a uniform connected with nursing and that he also had a link with another service which they specified as being the prison service. Bernard confirmed this.

At this stage of the sitting, spirit brought through the name of David, who was a very close family friend described as "a man of the cloth", which affected Bernard deeply as David had a special place in their family's affections. David gave evidence to prove his identity, reminding Bernard of the very special Christmas times which he had spent with him, Bernard's wife Ruth and their two daughters, and thanking them for the help and love they had shown him, and saying that he felt he could help Bernard with his present situation at work. David told Bernard that there was promotion ahead, and Bernard said he had applied for this but was very doubtful about the outcome as he felt problems might prevent this. However, spirit encouraged him to continue along these lines, because in spite of the problems, he would achieve the much deserved promotion as he was well able to do the job. Obviously this pleased Bernard who said he would definitely continue with it now, feeling more confident in the light of spirit's advice.

Bernard must have felt surprise when, a few months later, he was turned down for the promotion. He telephoned me to tell me, saying he still felt he should have got it and asking what he should do now. Spirit came through and advised him that the result was not final and he was still to go ahead and take it to a higher authority and not give up. Bernard said that

137

he had with him a letter he had just written to the appropriate authority but was not sure whether to send it. Now, in view of spirit's comments, he would go ahead and post it. Spirit still insisted that he would achieve this goal.

This all went completely out of my mind until I received a phone call from Bernard to say, "Thank you", and to thank everyone in spirit for their guidance and encouragement as after twelve months of fighting he had been given the promotion which spirit had assured him was possible. He was very glad that he had not given in to his own fears and had followed the guidance offered. At this point, Bernard's friend David gave me his name and wanted to say that he and Bernard's family in the spirit world were very pleased for him and that they had been sending out their love and prayers to help him and give him the confidence to continue, as they knew the result would be positive and that the promotion was there for him.

So you see, my friends, when those in the spirit world are sure of the correct pathway for the future of those they love on the earth plane, they never give up but continue with positive thoughts and guidance to encourage us, even when our own thoughts are negative and doubtful. They do not give in and make sure their voice is heard from the spirit world where they are "just a touch away".

Chapter Thirty

DOUBTS AND FEARS

Occasionally, stories are relayed back to us about things we are supposed to have done in the past which are amazing. Although they make me smile I can't help wondering how they came about. Of course, different people see us in different ways – to some we are workers for the devil, to others we are weird people who work in darkened rooms with lighted candles and clouds of burning incense; some people expect us to look like a pseudo-Romany, working with a crystal ball or some-such object, while others think mediums can read their minds and avoid us like the plague, or else come to the conclusion that we have a mental problem and talk to ourselves. It is sad that beliefs such as this still exist, but I hope that by writing and talking about the workings of spirit these misunderstandings will be cleared away and that more people will feel free to come to try to communicate with their loved ones.

One of the oddest stories I heard, was about a situation I was said to have created regarding some visitors to my home. The story went, that when the people told their neighbours they were coming to see me for a sitting, the response was, "I shouldn't if I were you. Didn't you hear what happened when two sisters went to see that medium?" It appears that after I gave them a sitting, I was supposed to have gone into another room, coming back after a while with a sealed envelope, which I gave to one of the sisters with strict instructions not to open it until returning to her home. On the way home the sisters were said to have been killed in a car accident and when the family opened the envelope it contained only a blank piece of paper; the point of the story being that I knew they were going to die. Since this story has been relayed to me by more than one person from a certain village, it is strange no report of any such accident nor evidence of any such ladies has come to light, particularly as the village is not far from where I live, and it definitely would have made news. Apparently, the originator was a very religious person who hoped to frighten people away from coming to see us, and each time the story was passed on, it grew.

Many people relate similar stories of being deterred from visiting us by friends or family who believed we work for the devil; some have even been told their friends or family will have nothing more to do with them if they come. However, when asked, sitters say it was worth it to receive the peace of mind they were searching for and that the people who "knock us" are afraid and do not know what they are missing. Most times, it is because these people have been indoctrinated into believing what they are told as being the absolute truth, and not given the chance to see the other side to the question. It is a pity they lack the courage to visit us to see for themselves, to be free to judge and comment from their own experience. Even my own cousin, who is a strong Jehovah's Witness, on knowing of my work told my family that they must have nothing to do with me and that I was evil. Thank goodness my family and friends know me better. Although some of them do not believe in spirit, they accept that it is my freedom of choice to do my chosen work, and as long as I do not try to impress my beliefs on them, that is fine with them, understanding that my only desire is to help and offer guidance to those who come freely to visit me.

Going back to people's attitudes and behaviour, I have even been told that visitors have been warned not to accept a drink before we begin the sitting, as I might put "something" in it – what I do not know – which might affect them and they will be "under my spell" and not know what is happening.

A while back, a lady came to me for a sitting and confirmed everything I was able to give her. She accepted it was her father who had communicated during her sitting and asked if, at a later date, she could book again and bring her brother with her. When the date arrived a few months later, the sitting was a disaster. Although their father came through with spasmodic information, it was all so disjointed that after trying for a while, I apologised to them and explained that I could not relate any more, and said I would not even charge them for the sitting although I had spent almost two hours trying to relate. It was obvious that they were disappointed.

A few weeks later, I received a letter from the lady, expressing her own and her brother's disappointment. It appears that the day of the sitting had been their father's birthday and also she herself was pregnant, and she had hoped he would have known, but nothing had been said about either. On talking to her friend about this, it was suggested that when she came to see me on her own, I was able to hypnotise her and read her mind, but when she came with her brother, I was unable to do this and therefore nothing had happened. After all this, she still felt she would like to come and see me for another sitting. I politely wrote back, explaining that I do not work that way and I cannot hypnotise anyone. If I could, I would probably be quite rich by now. That day had just been one of poor spirit communication and in circumstances where her father could not communicate properly, whether through his disability or mine. I would not make things up or tell them silly things; it had been much better to be honest and simply say I could not communicate. I suggested it might be better for her to contact a different medium who would perhaps get the results that she wished for.

Some time later, I did get another letter from the lady apologising. These letters are now on display in my home for people to read, as I believe in not just displaying the nice letters but also those which are a little bit sceptical, so that visitors can make up their own minds about my work with spirit. I am just here hoping to give evidence to the best of my ability to show that there is a life beyond this material plane to look forward to, and that those who have already gone over are "just a touch away" and able to communicate, giving knowledge, guidance and love from their world which is just beyond us.

Given the work we do connected to the world of spirit, it is never surprising to see the varied reactions to us from other people. Some totally accept our gift of spirit communication, others are totally opposed to it and attack it as being the work of the devil. I find it so very sad when people believe what they are told or have read, without investigating how it works before condemning it and broadcasting their comments far and wide. Very often, as a medium I come across these prejudices, but am glad that they do not bother me. Everyone has freedom of choice and I know that those who wish to see me will come, for these are the people I am here to help.

For me, it is the voice which is the important link with spirit, and once I connect with a person's voice, the vibrations needed are there, so I know when someone needs help and respond accordingly. A recent instance of communicating with a voice on the telephone, which made me query the reason for the call, was when a lady called asking how I worked. I explained that I was not a fortune-teller and could work only with what was given to me from spirit, being a medium working with those who have left us for the spirit world and passing evidence of their survival to those left behind. She asked to make bookings for three separate people on different days, all at 2.30 p.m. All this time, I had been aware of spirit making me curious about this lady, but I helpfully agreed to book them in, asking only the first names of the people concerned and entered them in the diary, thinking it strange that she neither asked my address nor how much I charged. On replacing the phone I was again aware that all was not right, so, as directed by spirit, I underlined each name with the date the booking was made and a question mark as to whether they would turn up.

Leaving it at that, I thought if spirit was right, then I would get some time to relax. Running Foot, my guide, was giving me the feeling that these ladies were of a particular religious belief and were hoping to block me by taking space so that others could not book in.

When the first date arrived, I noticed the comments in the diary and half-heartedly prepared myself for the sitting, but felt too relaxed which was strange, so I was intrigued to see whether spirit had been correct and would "tick me off" for not taking their word about this. True to form, the first lady did not turn up, so I was able to get on with other important issues which needed attention. Nobody telephoned. Also, the other two days were the same, so spirit once again showed me that I was being given the correct messages from them. Fortunately, a young man phoned just before 2.30 p.m. on the third day, so I was able to see him straightaway and give him the help and guidance he needed, so we didn't lose out, but gained, by helping someone in need. The people who were trying to hinder me in fact helped me, giving me a chance to have a break which I often need, and to recharge my batteries so that I can be strong to help others.

Even when people have phoned in and then somebody else arrives in their place, spirit will always make me aware and I usually remark on it, which tends to embarrass them, but it never bothers me as the person who does come often needs spirit help at that time rather than later, but it does surprise them that I can tune in so easily. For reasons such as these I can understand why so many people, not only family and friends, are wary of me and now I accept this as part of my chosen life of working with the spirit world.

It is also of benefit, because of people's awareness of my gift, I do find that I can trust those who come into my home. They are made to feel like "family", and I never worry about the others who are waiting outside for sittings as they are shown where to find the tea and coffee, and told to help themselves if they want another drink or wish to look at anything. I have never, so far, felt uneasy with anyone. Sometimes I even get them to help me by asking them to answer the phone and take messages, which they never seem to mind. If you are honest with people and treat them with respect, they tend to treat you in the same way. As long as we continue to use our gift in the right way, then no harm can ever be done and spirit will always guide me, giving me the confidence to continue with my communications with those from the world of spirit.

Chapter Thirty-one

NEVER ALONE

Following the departure of friends and loved ones for the world of spirit, we all have been known to say, "If only they were here now, they would help us." My friends, they can and will try.

We cry out for their love and help so often. During our everyday life, in the midst of crises such as problems with our children, our relationships or decision-making regarding changes in our lives, we long for their strength and guidance. Sometimes we may be dealing with something which seems trivial to other people but is important to us, and it prompts a yearning for help. We may accidently misplace or lose a very special memento of the person in spirit – maybe a piece of jewellery or a photograph which means a great deal to us – and we intuitively call to them for help, hoping to be pointed in the right direction or given an answer telling us where to search for the lost object.

I have included in this book a very recent happening which may, I hope, help others to try to reach out and build their own link with their special people in the spirit world.

It was during the month of November 1993, that a husband and wife made a return visit to my home to have a sitting, hoping for communication with their special son, who had left very quickly as the result of an accident seven years before. Once again, they were given love and reassurance from their son, who was in his early twenties when he left, that he was still part of their lives and still watching over them. He talked about how proud he was to now be an uncle, and about his brother's children and the other changes which had arisen since their previous visit to me nearly two years before.

Later in the afternoon, following their return home, I received a telephone call from this young man's mother, explaining that she had lost her engagement ring. She asked if I would look to see if it had fallen off where she had been sitting or perhaps when she had visited the bathroom. They had searched their own home several times and also their car, and retraced their steps to try to find it but all to no avail. Wishing to check thoroughly, I took their phone number and said I would get back to them when I had looked. Having searched every possible place where she could have dropped it, I had to ring back to say, "I'm sorry – no luck," and the lady was very upset. She had had this special ring for over thirty years and it could never be replaced.

Just as I was about to put the phone down, I was aware of giving her the following advice: I asked her to try to link up with her son and ask him for his help with the ring, as he might possibly be able to point her to its location. Ten minutes later, a very relieved and emotional lady phoned me back, saying that she had asked her son to help her, and for some reason was directed into the dining room which she was convinced she had gone over three times. She stopped inside the room and right in front of her, at her feet, was the ring. Her emotion was basically because her special son had been able to help her from spirit in her time of need and she could not thank us enough. However, the thanks was not really due to us but to her son who answered her call for help, which hopefully gave them extra proof that he is still there to help them and to keep the love flowing.

This incident is very similar in a way to something which happened to a friend of mine. This lady was divorced with five teenage children – one son and four daughters – and although the children's father had moved away and remarried, his stepfather had remained a very important figure in the children's lives.

The grandfather had given the girls pretty bracelets shortly before he died, suddenly and unexpectedly from a heart attack, leaving the girls feeling very bereft. They had mourned him deeply; to them he was a very important person and loved him dearly, and of course the bracelets were treasured.

One afternoon, one of the daughters named Rachel was in tears. She was wearing her precious bracelet, and on looking down, discovered that a piece was missing. To her, it mattered very much.

The house was searched unsuccessfully; the tiny piece could have been anywhere.

My friend decided to call the grandfather, Henry, to ask for his help in finding the missing piece. It was a long shot, but her daughter was distraught and it was worth a chance. "Please, Henry," she begged, "Please, if you can, help me find it – lead me to it."

She felt impressed to go out into the garden which was about seventy feet long and had quite long grass surrounded by shrubs and flower beds. She kept walking – and stopped. She looked down and nestling by her toe was the sparkling, tiny piece of her daughter's bracelet.

So, my friends, never be afraid to ask spirit yourself for their help and guidance. It may not always appear or happen as promptly as in this story – maybe the next day – but thoughts and ideas will be planted in your mind and the help or guidance you asked for, be given.

Chapter Thirty-two

RELIGION

In my previous books, I have told how often I am questioned regarding my own religious belief. People frequently ask me what spiritualists actually believe in, and whether we believe in God.

They seem genuinely astonished when I confirm that, not only do I believe in God, but daily thank him for the wonderful mediumistic gift which He has given me, and ask for help to use it to the best of my ability.

Many people are misled into believing that spiritualists do what is referred to as "the devil's work" – often by other religious groups who consider us evil but do not have the slightest idea about what we believe or what we actually do. Others who have taken the trouble to find out, learn of the help which is available through spiritualism (without interference in their lives), and are then in a position to decide for themselves whether or not it is right for them.

As I have stated, I do believe in God. I also believe, as my spirit family tells me it is true, that Jesus Christ was created in bodily form and came down to express God and his work, so that we here on the earth plane could relate to God. With regard to Jesus' role here on the earth plane, we are told (and the Bible states) that Jesus gave healing and hope to those sick in body and mind, brought people back from the dead, talked to God spiritually for love and guidance and also tried to inform people of things to come. He was condemned for all of this by people around him, and when Jesus finally left us for the world of spirit, He came back to show us that life continues in the world beyond.

Nowadays, we as spiritualists are continuing with God's work as Jesus Christ did, helping to heal the sick through spiritual healing and showing people that those who have left us for the world of spirit continue to live in the world beyond, showing that they can come back and relate to their loved ones and friends, not only sending their love but also offering guidance to help us who are still here on the earth plane. However, even in this day and age, we are also condemned by certain religions and it is still no different from the way it was in the beginning.

Spirit tells me that the Bible was created by man and man wrote as he saw and believed things to be; it is, therefore, open to question. I find it very sad, therefore, when many religious fanatics can only quote the Bible as absolute truth, feeling it cannot be doubted or questioned, refusing to consider anything apart from what is written. Obviously, I believe in continuing life after we have left this earth plane and try to demonstrate that truth which is for all people, no matter what beliefs they may hold.

Every religion offers something, but each person needs freedom of choice to search for the religious pathway which is most suitable and no one should dictate to another what is or is not right for them. There is a great difference between following a religion which is a true expression of your own inner beliefs and being brainwashed into doing so by leaders who scare you into thinking they alone have the truth and that you will be damned for ever if you explore any other possibilities. God is much greater than that and is infinitely more loving. Those with open minds are free to think and explore for themselves, but established religions tend to reject such people because they are a threat to the structure of their rigid belief systems, and obviously are also disruptive to the monopoly of power held by the leaders.

God is God, no matter how he is seen or perceived by people of different races, times or culture. What is important is that He is, that we are all part of Him, and that He loves us all. No matter what any of us chooses to do with our life here on earth, we have freedom of choice as to belief and action, and should use that responsibility wisely. We shall, no doubt, understand more when we get to spirit and be able to put all our earth experiences to good use, as indeed our loved ones and friends already in spirit are now doing, as they come to offer help and guidance to us. Hopefully, as we progress together, a more peaceful and understanding future will become possible for us all.

At one time when one branch of the Christian church was forcefully expressing their disagreement with what local spiritualists were doing, a friend of mine wrote the following letter to show what she felt. For any of you who have experienced being on the receiving end of such misunderstanding, it may be an encouragement to read. We are not alone.

Dear Jesus,
    You seem to be a bit busy on the telephone, so I thought I would write. I am so sorry for you when I hear all this carry-on between some of your people and others who are seeking to live a spiritual life and develop their contact with the Source of all things.
    The fear and bitterness are amazing. What is it all about? I presume you must be in a position to know all the "ins and

outs" of the conflict and I should be most grateful to know what you think about it. Not from them – from you. Is that possible, do you think?

Because hearing a calm, sane voice speaking in this mêlée is almost impossible. People are speaking entirely from their own individual points of view and claiming they speak for you. How do you feel about that? There are so many men and women claiming to know you personally and know exactly what your position is on every subject, but it's a funny thing that you never say anything to any of them that is out of line with their own particular belief system. Why is that?

I've tried looking at it all sorts of ways. Looked at historically, I can see that whenever anyone has believed anything different from the crowd, however accurate that new belief has proved to be, the crowd has either hauled him up before the courts, persecuted him, tortured him, burned him at the stake or crucified him. I believe you know a bit about that?

And as for people of different religions? Well, I always thought God was the creator of *all* creation. I didn't realise that he had only created one particular in-group of the Christian church, excluding all the other kinds of Christian believers, all men and women of other faiths and all the natural cosmos. If that is true, could you let me know as soon as possible who God's boss is, because obviously I'll have to be getting into touch with him about all this. Was I wrong, by the way, about your being born a Jew? Or doesn't that count? I suppose there weren't too many Christian women around to choose from, when God chose your mother to bring you into this world for him. I guess he found her acceptable to be his partner and your mother even if she wasn't in a position to be a Christian. By the way, if only evangelical Christians go to heaven when they die, what about your Dad – Joseph – for instance? He must have been pretty well thought of by God presumably. Where is he these days?

As for talking to the dead, incidentally, like these spiritualists and people, well, of course, everyone knows that's not possible. Why did *you* do it, Jesus? Some of your people tell me it is a sin. I thought you were sinless. Or perhaps you were just pretending to talk to Moses and Elijah on that mountain, were you? I mean, they couldn't hear anyway, could they? And no doubt your disciples were hallucinating when they saw them with you. What's more, since you yourself died, when people do that praying stuff and talk to you, well, you can't hear either, can you? And then there is this healing business, whoever heard of people being cured of anything just by "loving them better" or putting your hands on the bits that hurt. Fancy anyone believing that – oh, well, I know you could do it and I know you said, "What I can do, you can do too"; perhaps you were talking to a group of mothers at the time, they do it continually.

I know what they'll tell me. I *know* what the Bible says – it has some of the most beautiful teaching I have ever read – but I know too that you felt free to update some of the material in it that you knew was out of date and said, "But, I say unto you . . . " And you're sinless, as I said, so I needn't be afraid of following your example and knowing what my heart knows.

That prostitute you spent a lot of time with, Jesus, and that spy-like tax collector fellow who was a friend of yours, some of the religious people around you didn't think too much of your being so pally with them, did they? Perhaps they thought you should have spent more time with them. Why was that, by the way, what were the qualities you were looking for in your friends? You really didn't seem very interested in whether they were religious or not. Much more interested in whether they were loving – and what was that you said about people worshipping God in spirit and in truth? Sounds awfully like some of those unacceptable psychic types talking – they're always going on about love and truth and cosmic law and stuff. I expect the rumours may be right – they are probably possessed by evil spirits.

But then, they said you were possessed by the Devil, didn't they?

With much love.

M.

Chapter Thirty-three

CHURCHES

Over the years I have been working with spirit, a surprising number of people have approached me to find out more about spiritual things and wishing to have more information about spiritualist churches. Often people are under the impression that only spiritually-aware people can attend spiritualist services and events, even thinking that one needs an invitation to do so, or to be accompanied by a member of the church. They seem genuinely surprised to be told that anybody is welcome in our church, no matter what religion they belong to, as the spiritualist church is for everyone, the purpose not being to tell everybody what to believe, but to show us that life continues beyond death and to offer help and guidance.

Another question which is frequently asked is, "Well, what actually goes on in spiritualist churches?" I am sure many are waiting for me to say that it is all very mysterious with darkened windows and flickering candles, with the smell of incense everywhere. I tell them, in fact, that it is run on lines similar to other churches, but to me more cheerful, friendly, and more like a family evening together. At the close of the service, there is a welcome cup of tea and a biscuit for whoever is not in a mad rush to get home or with a train to catch, with people free to chat and ask questions of the medium or church members. I must admit that I have been at a church where those in charge cannot wait to get everyone out as quickly as possible, and I've ended up talking to people in the street, but thank goodness this happens very rarely.

The thing which is different from orthodox churches is that during services, instead of listening to a sermon from the vicar, the time is spent listening to a medium passing on messages to members of the congregation from friends and loved ones whose funerals were last week, last year, or twenty years before. A kind of telephone exchange, if you like – or a radio station, broadcasting messages from one state to another. Closed minds say, "But that's impossible". Open minds say, "But we do it every day."

During the week, there are meetings where people learn how to develop spiritually and psychically, practising using their own abilities to hear or see or sense spirit people and to communicate with them clearly and accurately. It is not at all spooky; there is a lot of laughter, cheerfulness and fun.

Spiritualism is the name given to a religion formalised óver one hundred years ago, to express the natural abilities of man's soul, such as spiritual healing, prophecy, talking with spirits and understanding what happens to people beyond the death of the body.

Many articles and books have been written about the history of the spiritualist movement in America and Britain, about the wonderful events which have shaped its progress, and about the famous men and women who have acted as mediums for spiritual communication of all kinds throughout the years.

Spiritualism is a religion as man-made as any other. Religions belong on earth; nothing so divisive is needed in a perfect heaven, but the whole focus of spiritualism is to demonstrate the survival of the human spirit beyond physical death. Other religions and philosophies offer many things, but this is the particular contribution of spiritualism. As, however, there are many different kinds of people with differing needs of self-expression, so there are different kinds of spiritualist churches. This puzzles many people who wonder why there are sub-divisions even within the spiritualist movement, but spiritualists are human, just like anybody else and feel at home with different backgrounds.

Mediums have been around, though called by different names, for thousands of years, from cultures as wide apart as Ancient Greece, Africa and the Americas. The knowledge was not a religion, but a part of life. Ancient Egyptians, Aborigines, Red Indians and Celts have proclaimed, "Life goes on." However, it was not until the middle of the nineteenth century that the spiritualist movement began.

In 1750, Franz Mesmer was experimenting on the continent with healing rods under conditions which apparently induced trance in his subjects, during which they demonstrated unusual phenomena; as did du Patet in France later. Andrew Jackson Davis wrote a book in 1847, which was dictated in trance, on spiritual matters, and the medium Emmanuel Swedenborg was writing on such subjects as long ago as the end of the seventeenth century. However, it was not until 1848 that modern spiritualism is considered to have begun. Various groups were formed and newspapers printed, but the movement did not become truly national until 1890 with the "birth" of the Spiritualist National Union. Today there are many S.N.U. churches throughout the country existing alongside those of the Greater World Christian Spiritualist League, started in 1931, as well as many independent churches. The main difference between the S.N.U. and the Greater World churches has to do with the divinity (as against humanity) of Jesus Christ, and the independent churches do not wish to avoid taking personal responsibility for their beliefs and actions.

From my own experience, every church has its own personality – some more adventurous than others, some richer, some more progressive, some rigid and afraid of change. When asked, rather than forcing my own opinions on people, I try to give a balanced view of good and doubtful points and what to seek or avoid.

When someone questioning me wants to take their curiosity further, I try to provide details of the nearest spiritualist church with address and times of service, and if possible, will introduce them to the church or members so they do not feel strange or out of place. I can truthfully say that in the majority of churches I have attended either as speaker or a member of the congregation, I have always received a very warm, friendly welcome. Sadly, there have been the odd few who have frowned when I have served the church, because I never wear a suit, collar or tie. To me, when I work, I have to feel relaxed and comfortable, otherwise I am not at my best. I always make certain that I dress tidily and casually, but I know that in the beginning of my spiritual work, comments were passed about this, although never to my face. Some of the older members want to keep everything in a time capsule, not allowing new people to have a voice in case changes are made of which they disapprove. I have occasionally heard the odd grumble if a child cries or wanders about. What we have to remember is that these children will be the future of the spiritualist church and continue when we have taken our journey into the spirit world.

Many churches hold very happy memories for me – a genuine welcome, a cup of tea, the offer of any hymns I would like sung and so on. Some, knowing that I am not all that keen on giving an address, will even allow me to go straight into giving clairvoyance, but I am aware that some churches do not book me because of this, which I find a little sad as it is those who attend the church who then lose out.

At one church, when I first began my work on the platform, I became very irritated by being taken into a back room before the service where I was questioned and given instructions on what I might and might not do in their church. I felt like putting on my coat and going home. Suddenly, I became aware of Running Foot talking to me with the message, "Calm down. It's not the church or those that run it that are important, it is the people who attend the church who need spirit's help and guidance who are important." This is something I have never forgotten and now, when I serve a church with rigid restrictions and bossy people, I just smile and get on with it, remembering the boss' words.

This experience, fortunately, is not a frequent one, and although I prefer not to serve churches with a "high and mighty" attitude, I know this is not in accordance with Running Foot's feelings. I do feel that in order to work harmoniously with spirit in churches, the harmony should exist within the church also, and we need a happy and relaxed atmosphere to work with our spirit friends.

Many churches have special love in them. As mediums, we just turn up, give our services, and go home. The unsung heroes are those who selflessly devote time and energy to making the work a success. These people have the daunting task of keeping a church running, suffering the frustrations of ensuring everyone is happy and hopefully working in harmony with each other, making sure the medium is booked and at ease, trying to organise special events, teaching, maintaining funding to keep the church running, and then often being blamed for everything that goes wrong. I salute these people. Without them there would be no churches, and they should be thanked and recognised more often for their valuable contribution to spirit.

It is very difficult to single out any special church, but one I should like to include in my book is The Temple of Living Spirit at Boston, where I serve as a medium, but also attend whenever I can as a member of the congregation. To me it radiates happiness. It is held in the church hall adjoining the Unitarian Church. It is an independent church, originally formed by Dawn Perkins, but due to Dawn's resignation in the Spring of 1992, was doomed to be closed down. Along came Monica Harrison and Paul Underwood, who, with no knowledge of running a church, took on the task, renamed it The Temple of Living Spirit, and with the help of the members, took it from there. It has gone from strength to strength, and although numbers vary, services are well attended; it has a closed circle, an open development circle and a good healing group. On top of this, when the hall is available, Monica is on the look-out to have seminars, teachings and special events, not only to raise funds but to keep everyone involved in the church interested. Having been lucky enough to watch this church progress, it is good to see regular members turn up early to assist with setting out the room ready for the service, and the number of young people, including young men, who have shown an interest over the past year, coming on a regular basis to learn more about spirit. I think what makes this church stand out from others is the special greeting everyone receives – everyone gets a nice, big hug and a welcome. No one is left to stand on their own, and after the service, no one ever seems in a hurry to leave; the room is full of chatter and laughter during refreshment time, and when you finally leave, you leave with another friendly hug and go home feeling on top of the world; the feeling lasts for days. I wish all churches could create this loving atmosphere, but some are getting there. It just needs people to learn to relax and to be themselves. Maybe that is the secret – there you are accepted for just exactly whatever you are – and it is a good experience.

Another factor which makes churches special is the singing. Many churches lack the sound of voices singing loudly and freely and people seem to be unable to enjoy themselves. Some hymns, of course, leave a lot to be desired, but where there is joyful singing, the whole atmosphere of the church changes and you may depend upon the fact that spirit will always respond.

There is another very special church where this is in abundance and this is Whitham Road Spiritualist Church, Sheffield. The committee and church members are some of the friendliest people I have ever come into contact with and I feel I can never wait for my next visit. These special Yorkshire people have a special place in my heart. They certainly raise the roof with their singing. Even before the service begins, they arrive up to an hour early so that they can all join in the sing-song with Bill leading the singing, Dorothy on the organ. Everyone is well away and the vibrations in the church are so high before the medium reaches the rostrum, spirit is already in tune to come through with their love and messages. To me, this church is a family church – not only with Bill, Dorothy and cheeky Mary pulling everyone's leg, but the rest of the committee and congregation stand out way in front of others with warmth, love and harmony. I only wish I could mention so many more of the lovely churches who have kindly booked me over the last few years and from whom I hope for many years of continued friendship, but it would need a whole book devoted to them, so I hope that I am forgiven.

All churches vary, so do go along and see for yourselves. If you are unsure about the first one you try, there are many more around. I know they will make you welcome in their own individual way and answer any questions you may have. If ever you meet me in church, please come and say "Hello". It will be good to meet you on our way to "Spirit – our Second Home".

DEATH IS NOTHING AT ALL

Death is nothing at all
I have only slipped away
Into the next room.
I am I, and you are you.
Whatever we were to each
Other, that we are still.

Call me by my old familiar name.
Speak to me in the easy
Way which you always used.
Put no difference into your tone;
Wear no forced air of
Solemnity or sorrow.

Laugh, as we always laughed
At the little jokes we enjoyed
Together. Play, smile, think of me.
Pray for me.
Let my name be ever
The household word that it always was.

Let it be spoken without affect,
Without the ghost of a shadow on it.
Life means all that it ever meant;
It is the same as it ever was.

There is absolutely unbroken
Continuity. What is this death
But a negligible accident?
Why should I be out of mind
Because I am out of sight?

I am but waiting for you
For an interval –
Somewhere very near,
Just around the corner.
All is well.

Canon Holland of St. Paul's.